Beyond Pocahontas

Beyond Pocahontas

by

Sandra Waugaman

The Dietz Press

Published by The Dietz Press
Richmond, Virginia
www.dietzpress.com

Photography by Sandra Waugaman

ISBN-13: 978-0-87517-134-0
ISBN-10: 0-87517-134-6
Library of Congress Control Number: 2007929205

Sandra Foulis Waugaman

This book is dedicated to the memory of author Sandra Waugaman. Even though I only knew Mrs. Waugaman for a few years, she and her husband Si were a blessed influence on our family. I admired her passion, tenacity, and

Sandra Foulis Waugaman

perfection as a writer. In her book *We're Still Here* and also in this new book, she has given to the Native people of Virginia a voice that has been buried and forgotten for so long. Her perfection was seen through the numerous notes and recordings as well as phone calls to make sure that each life-story, each statement, each historical fact was correct. She wanted the truth to be revealed.

I also admired Mrs. Waugaman for another profession that she held — that of a tender mother. When she told me the story about her son Craig and how she cared for him during his illness until his death at the age of 34, as a mother I was moved by her unconditional love and her fighting spirit that drove her and held her family together. The death of a child is the hardest situation a mother can know. Family has always been the foundation or focal point among Native people. In the pages of this book, you will read stories of women who are carrying on the passed-down traditions of their families and their people, written from the heart of a woman who understands just how precious and priceless a family is.

The absence of Mrs. Waugaman's talent, passion, and laughter are a great loss, but because of her love and dedication, the true life-stories of Virginia Indians will continue to be read and heard for many generations to come. I consider it an honor and a privilege to have called her my friend.

Kelly "Autumn Dove" Adkins

Contents

✳

Introduction

✳

Although she lives only in our imaginations and media presentations now, Pocahontas is one of the most well-known American Indian women in our history. It is often said that without her help, and the help of others in the Powhatan Nation, those who stepped ashore on the banks of the James River in 1607 would not have survived to make Jamestown the first permanent English settlement in the New World.

As important as members of those Powhatan tribes were, there are not many who know their names. The Cuttatawomen and Pissaseck have faded into history, just as many think all of the early tribes of indigenous people have. But the descendants of several of the early tribes still live in the areas that they lived in when John Smith led parties of Englishmen through the woods of Virginia. Two of these tribes, the Pamunkey and the Mattaponi, still retain their reservations, and six other tribes are officially recognized by the state. Seven of these tribes, the Chickahominy, Eastern Chickahominy, Rappahannock, Nansemond, Upper Mattaponi, Mattaponi, and Pamunkey were connected with the great Chief Powhatan and all were Eastern Woodland tribes who were united by the Algonquian language. They inhabited Coastal and Central Virginia. The eighth state-recognized tribe, the Monacan Nation, is located in the western part of the state, and its members spoke a Siouan dialect.

As the permanence of English colonies in North America became a reality, their maps used an Indian woman to symbolize the area. An Indian princess joined a tropical Indian queen representing South America on a map by Henry Popple created in London in 1733. In the Library of Congress's collection on American Women, they picture the cartouche from Henry Popple's *Map of the British Empire in America with the French and Spanish settlements adjacent thereto*. The caption reads, "The tropical Indian queen surveys her world from above the map title. Surrounded by a palm tree, an alligator, a parrot, and a monkey... she announces her South American origins. To the right, her daughter, the Indian princess, represents the British Colonies in North America...."

It could be surmised from this that the English recognized the importance of Indian women to their communities. Among the Algonquian-speaking Indians in the area now consisting of Eastern and Central Virginia and parts of North Carolina, Indian women were the backbone of their communities. Theirs was a matriarchal society, with the children's lineage determined by the tribal association of the mother. The women owned the property and assets and were instrumental in the governing of their tribes. Two of the signers of the 1677 Treaty of Middle Plantation were women. A Pamunkey woman, Cockacoeske signed as "Queen Pomunckey on behalfe of herselfe and the severall Indians under her Subjection." The Queen of the Weyonoke also signed the treaty. In 1715 Queen Ann of the Pamunkeys went to Governor Spotswood on behalf of her nation to request fair treatment for her people.

In 1607 in Central and Coastal Virginia, there were 32 to 34 tribes under the rule of Chief Powhatan. Over the years interpretations of his name have changed. It was always known that Wahunsunacock (some now spell it Wahusenacawh) was his Indian name. Now historians say it was the personal, or first name, of the chief of a tribe known as the Powhatans who took the name of his tribe as his throne name. So the name Powhatan was used for the supreme ruler of a group of tribes, for a specific tribe on the banks of the river near what is now Richmond, and also for the river currently called the James River.

His daughter, Pocahontas, was called Matoaca by her people. Throughout the years and in various accounts, there are several different meanings and spellings given for her name. One, a web source www.nativearts.com, lists her as a Pamunkey Indian born around 1595, who died in 1617 at Graves End in England. They say Pocahontas is from the Algonquian "pocahantesu" which translates to "She is Playful."

Another translation suggests "Bright Stream Between Two Hills." Matoaca or Mataoaka is also spelled Matoax or Matowaka. That name is said to translate to "She Plays with Things." Both Pocahontas and Matoaca can be said to refer to her vivacious disposition.

Still another source, Dr. Dennis A. J. Morey, says her tribal name was Amanute, Matoax or Matoaca, and Pocahontas was a nickname meaning "little wanton" or "little mischief."

Most agree she was probably born at Werowocomoco, Powhatan's capital, to one of Powhatan's 30 wives and was one of her father's favorites.

What we know of her short life was remarkable. In John Smith's writings she was credited with bringing food to the settlers in the stockaded settlement, thus helping them survive in the New World.

On a trip to the northern part of the state, she was captured by the English and taken to Henricus, the second English settlement. Henricus was established by Sir Thomas Dale in 1611. He led a group from Jamestown with instructions from the Virginia Company to find an area with a healthier environment as well as a location that would be easier to defend from the Indians and Spanish. It was there that Pocahontas met John Rolfe, her future husband. Under the tutelage of the Reverend Alexander Whitaker, she converted to Christianity and took the English name of Rebecca. She was baptized in 1614. After her marriage to Rolfe, they moved to his plantation, Varina, which was across the river from Henricus, and there she gave birth to a son they named Thomas.

Throughout history Pocahontas has been held up as a model of the American Indian or Native American woman. Just as there is disagreement among some contemporary Indians as to whether they should be called Native Americans, American Indians, or First People, there are currently a few Virginia Indians who question her role as an Indian heroine. To them her conversion to Christianity was a betrayal of her people and her heritage. Others contend that she was not betraying her people, rather that she was acting as a spy for her father, trying to find out as much as she could about the English who had invaded their territory. The real truth about her life and actions may never be known, because she was never able to record them herself, as her people did not have a written language. Most of what we know about her comes from the writings of the early English, and they did not always understand Indian rituals or actions. As the years have passed, these early writings have also been embellished and altered to suit the advertising and entertainment industry needs.

Beyond the myths about Pocahontas, beyond the questionable stories of her relationship with John Smith, and beyond her portrayal in movies, there are many contemporary Virginia Indian women who are still carrying on the traditions and culture of her people.

Chapter 1

❋

Chief G. Anne Richardson
Rappahannock Tribal Leader

It was dark under the table, and eight-year-old Anne Nelson pulled her legs in tighter to make herself as small as possible so that no one would find her hiding place. Soon the Rappahannock tribal council members would take their

seats at the dining room table in the Nelson house. Each time someone sat down she was afraid that they might stretch out their legs and bump her with a foot. She knew that children were not allowed at Tribal Council meetings, but her father was the chief and she was curious about the things that he did.

Looking back she says, "Daddy had such an exciting life, and I wanted to be there for every part of it. They would have the council meetings in my home. I was always very curious but never allowed in the room during the meeting, so that was why I would hide under the table before they came in. And it's a good thing that I did because that was where I heard the story of state registrar Walter Plecker. I

Chief G. Anne Richardson in her office at MPM.

couldn't believe that he had admired Adolph Hitler, and corresponded with some of the Nazis. The council felt that Plecker was a fierce enemy of the tribes because he would not allow "Indian" to be shown as a person's race on any state documents."

What she heard that night surprised and shocked her. It upset her so much that the next day she went to her mother and asked if what she had heard could possibly be true.

She says, "My mother had taught me who Adolph Hitler was and told me stories she remembered from growing up during WWII. She had such sympathy for the Jewish people. She would sit and watch programs about the war on TV and cry. And she told me that, while he was not killing Indians like Hitler was killing Jews, Walter Plecker was trying to destroy us by denying our identity."

What Plecker did has been called documentary genocide, and while political policies have been corrected, the results of his practices are still difficult for many to deal with. As an adult and now chief of the Rappahannock tribe, Chief Richardson says, "That period created trauma that has impacted native people for generations, but I believe exposure is the path to healing. However; it has to be done very carefully and it has to be done when people are ready."

As she says, "I grew up in a politically savvy environment and was taught about current events and what they meant to us. I remember the Civil Rights Movement well. My mother would watch television with me and provide commentary on each issue. She was a wonderful teacher and taught me so much, not only about the present, but also about our past. She was one of our tribal historians. I was very blessed; she was a traditional Indian woman and she taught me and others that lived around us our history and ways. She shared her lifetime of learning with us. My Uncle Jim also taught us the old ways. He taught all the community children to dance, and he headed our dance group. When we grew up, dancing and drumming were the things you did. The tribe had some property and every spring the men would go down there and clear the grounds. Uncle Jim would bring in the drum, and he and my Aunt Doris taught us the dances. They poured their whole lives into our tribe and perpetuating the history and culture of our people. My father and mother also worked with the people who created Jamestown Settlement to make the recreated Powhatan Village accurate. My parents, aunts Doris and Ethel, and Uncle Jim were some of the first interpreters of that area."

By the time Anne was 15 she was working with her father typing letters for him and attending meetings. When she was 24 she was elected assistant chief, a position she occupied for eighteen years until she was elected chief in 1998. At that time she became the first woman chief in Virginia since the 1700s. Now she leads a tribe of approximately 300 people.

The Rappahannock tribe has always been a matrilineal tribe, one where kinship is derived through the mother and the assets of the family pass through the mother's side. There have always been women on the tribal council, and women play a major role in the tribe. As Chief Richardson says, "Women have always had strong leadership roles in our tribe, either formally or informally. In the past we had two queens."

Her parents always referred to the various families as clans, and each one had a clan mother who was knowledgeable about tribal genealogy and family history.

Chief Richardson cites this example, "When I married, my grandmother was a clan mother. My aunts, on my mother's side of the family - not my father's side, but my mother's side - had to check out my intended husband. They had to investigate him genealogically to insure that I was not marrying into a family clan that was too closely related. The clan mothers controlled all that and still exert a degree of power over those things."

She goes on to say, "Recently I heard a conversation between two clan mothers who were kind of strategizing about who would be married to whom, and the kids were only 12 or 13 years old. But they were saying 'we're facilitating that marriage', and they were creating opportunities for our women to marry other Indian men."

L. to R. Faye Fortune, Secretary of the Rappahannock Tribe with Chief Richardson outside the Rappahannock Tribal Center.

The Rappahannock's history has been preserved by the clan mothers and other leaders of the tribe. They have a written history that they share with other people, but it is not traditional for them to share their oral history with outsiders.

Some of the written history was recorded by Frank Speck, who spent a great deal of time with the tribe and was made an honorary member. Speck was a well known anthropologist, who was the chairman of the Department of Anthropology at the University of Pennsylvania. He died in 1950, but there are still members of the tribe who remember his visits.

Chief Richardson says, "I think what historians have missed is that the land was very spread out, and tribal people went where there were resources when they needed them. They were cyclical people who worked in conjunction and coordination with the seasons. So in the summer we would be on the Rappahannock River where we could fish, trap turtles, and grow corn. Then in the winter we reverted back to this ridge line which is about three miles from the river. It would have been nothing for the people to move three miles to this high ridge that would have protected them from the weather during the winter.

This area would also have provided plenty of game to sustain them. They were smart. They had summer homes and winter homes. Their homes were mats placed over a sapling frame. It was no trouble to take the mats off the frame, and take them with them to cover the frames they had left in another area."

The area now occupied by the Rappahannocks and the location of their tribal center is King and Queen County, Virginia. The thick woods with its underground springs and many streams and ponds have been home to many beavers over the years. Perhaps that is why long ago the beaver was chosen as

Chief Richardson in her regalia wearing the turkey feather crown that was worn by chiefs in the Powhatan Empire.

the symbol of the tribe, and they are called the Beaver Clan. Chief Richardson says, "Beavers built many homes here, and so did the Rappahannock. It's interesting that many of the characteristics of beavers can be applied to our tribe. For one thing, beavers work together as a team, and they don't allow anyone or anything to stop them from getting what they want built. A few years ago a wildlife magazine did a study on beavers and listed all their different characteristics, and I could pick out the same characteristics of our tribe."

Chief Richardson has initiated several projects to help not only the Rappahannocks but all native people. She was one of the founders of the United Indians of Virginia (UIV). Along with Warren Cook and Marvin Bradby, they

L. to R. in back – Gladys Nelson, Chief Richardson's mother, her Uncle Jim Ware, and Aunt Doris Ware were among the first interpreters in the recreated Powhatan Village at Jamestown Settlement.

formed a group where the chiefs could come together in council, make decisions, and then pass those decisions on to the governor through the Virginia Council on Indians.

She was also one of the organizers of Native American Advocates Against Violence. The goal of that organization is to educate people and teach them non-violent methods of conflict resolution. The organization grew out of Women's Conferences that she held to help women learn to identify the potential for violence and recognize the stages of conflict which can escalate into violence. She felt that it was important for women to come together and talk about these issues because women who are empowered are less likely to be controlled by others, and she feels violence is all about control.

In addition, Chief Richardson is the National Chairperson of the Secretary of Labor's Advisory Council on Indian and Native American Programs. Also, the Library of Virginia honored her as one of the eight outstanding women for the 2006 Virginia Women in History program.

She adds, "I've always been active in the Native American community in general. I've been with the Mattaponi, Pamunkey and Monacan, Inc. organization

Chief Richardson and assistant chief Mark Fortune lead the Grand Entry at a Rappahannock powwow.

(or MPM) for 20 years and am now the executive director. The goal of that organization is to find jobs and training for Indians. We send students to community colleges to get their associate degrees or to update their skills, depending on what they want to do. MPM has produced a chiropractor, nurses, business managers, and computer technicians."

Her father, Chief Emeritus Captain O. Nelson, died in the spring of 2003. He lived to see his daughter become chief and his tribe receive state recognition in 1983. She remembers he cried when he heard that. He was so happy that, after years of fighting to keep the state from denying them their birthright, they had finally received an acknowledgment of who they were.

Until his death he was hoping that the tribes would also receive federal recognition. Tribes that greeted and helped the English settlers who landed at Jamestown are still not recognized by the federal government even though their treaties predate the establishment of the United States.

While most historians cite 1606 as the first contact between the English and Virginia Indians, a Rappahannock historian is researching an earlier contact in 1603 between Samuel Mace and the Rappahannock tribe. Evidently Mace was sent by Sir Walter Raleigh to look for the settlers who founded the colony at Roanoke Island in North Carolina but were gone when their supply ship returned. The fate of those from the Lost Colony is still a mystery, but the connection of Virginia Indians with those from the rest of the world is not.

Chief Richardson enjoys relating a story of a visit from Indians from Bolivia in 2004. A group of Bolivian singers called Kalamarka was visiting Washington, D. C., and wanted to visit a Native American tribe near Washington. Consequently, they called the Bureau of Indian Affairs and received contact information for the Rappahannocks. When they visited, Chief Richardson was in the midst of developing a pictorial exhibit for their tribal center. She says, "They had a Spanish interpreter with them, but he couldn't understand their tribal language too well and when they saw a picture taken in the early 20's of Rappahannock women standing in front of a tribal quilt they all began talking and pointing. Finally the interpreter figured out what they were saying and said, 'They want to know where you got their tribal flag from.' I said that's not your tribal flag; that's our tribal quilt pattern. 'Oh, no that's our tribal flag,' they repeated. They showed me a DVD they had with a picture of their tribal flag on it. I was amazed. They were right; it was the same, so they wanted to come to our tribal powwow. They contacted their Bolivian dancers, and they did come to our powwow. Our people were a little concerned, however, about dancing to their music, saying 'These guys play pan flutes. How are we going to dance to pan flute music?' And I said, 'You know what, it doesn't matter. There's such a connection here that it doesn't matter; it's going to work out.' Well, they danced first, and they began to do what they said was their war dance. We couldn't believe it - it was our rabbit dance! So since one of our dances was exactly the same as theirs, there was absolutely no problem dancing to pan flute music."

She adds, "I think that speaks to the fact that it really is a small world, and how in the past the tribes did not have the borders that we have today. As native people we don't acknowledge the borders, they weren't our borders, we didn't put them there to begin with, and we don't have to adhere to them."

Chapter 2

Tammy D. Jefferson
Chickahominy Bead Worker

"Five turquoise beads, three yellow, and then five more turquoise ones." Fourteen-year-old Courtney Wynn checks the graph of her beadwork design frequently as she works at the beading loom under the watchful eye of her Aunt Tammy. Courtney learned how to do beadwork in special classes that the Chickahominy tribe used to have for their young people on Saturdays. The children called it "Indian School." She says, "It was a program on Saturday mornings till midday. We had three classes and a little lunch break. We learned pottery, leather work and beadwork. With beads we made bracelets and necklaces, and in leather work we made an array of objects from wallets to purses and knife pouches. People could progress to making regalia with the skills they learned there. Once you work with the leather you become more familiar with it – and also the beads. It was mostly elementary and middle school kids, and they probably weren't ready for a project as big as regalia, so it was

Tammy made the beaded appliquéd crown that the 2006 Junior Miss Chickahominy, Ashton Montez, wears.

Tammy talks to a customer at her booth at the VITAL powwow at the Chickahominy Tribal Grounds.

mostly accessories that we made. But it was something that made us authentic. We also learned a few words and numbers in the Algonquian language although our language is really gone now. Some days classes were cut short and we would learn traditional Indian dances."

A couple of years ago funds ran out for those classes. Once the classes were over, many of the children stopped using the skills they had learned, but Courtney wanted to keep up her beadwork. She says, "Aunt Tammy does beadwork a lot, and I think her work is really pretty. Since we don't have classes any more, I asked her to show me things because I didn't want to lose my ability to do beadwork. I wanted to get back into the habit of doing it. I made red and blue earrings from a pattern she taught me, and I taught my younger sister Taylor to make some too."

Courtney adds, "When you choose the beads you are going to use, you can make things that all match – earrings, bracelets and necklaces. We can wear them with our regular clothes, and they really dress things up. When I wear them to school people say, 'Oh, I love your earrings. They're so pretty. Where did you get them?' And they can't believe it when I tell them I made them."

The tie she is doing on the loom as a Father's Day present for her dad is the most ambitious project she has undertaken yet. She drew up the design herself on special beading graph paper. She says, "I wanted a turtle because that's the symbol of our tribe, and I wanted something round for all the directions of the earth, and a feather.

Some of Tammy's beadwork and supplies.

Then I added a cursive "R" because my dad's name is Roger and repeated the design again. Turtle, circle, feather. Aunt Tammy showed me how to work out the design because she does all her own designs."

Tammy says, "Most of the time I make up my own designs, but sometimes I see other beaded things that I like and change them a little to make them my own."

She adds, "The beading that our ancestors did was mostly with shells, antlers, pieces of bone, or animal claws and teeth along with clay or copper beads. Copper was a big thing, as that meant wealth. Chief Powhatan wore a lot of copper. They also used wampum which came from a clam shell. Wampum was used for decoration but was more widely known for its use as money and for barter. It wasn't until the English came that we saw glass beads and traded for them. That's why sometimes they were called trade beads. They were bigger than the tiny glass beads we use now, and Indians used a bone needle along with animal sinew for the thread. My Great Uncle Van made the necklace I wear with my regalia, and he used pieces of a deer's antler, seeds, and clay beads that he made himself.

My husband hunts, and he will use sinew and string bone to make necklaces. His brother also hunts, and once he came across a dead beaver. He made my husband a necklace of the beaver claws with handmade wooden beads.

We can wear animal parts: claws, bone, fur, teeth and things like that in our

Tammy helps her niece Courtney pick up beads for her work on the loom.

Tammy Jefferson works on an appliquéd barrette similar to the finished one in the foreground.

Examples of Tammy's beadwork using wampum as the centerpiece.

The barrette Tammy made for Jessica Canaday to wear in her hair when she turned her beaded crown over to the next Miss Chickahominy.

Close up of Tammy Jefferson working on an appliquéd barrette.

Courtney Wynn working on the tie for her father on the beading loom.

Courtney with some beads for her project.

Courtney Wynn counts and picks up beads for the tie she is making her father.

Courtney Wynn wears the beaded earrings she made.

Close-up of a beaded bolo tie Tammy made.

regalia, but you're not supposed to intentionally kill an animal to get their parts, and you can't sell them. One year, I don't know if it was a Virginia Game and Fish Department person or some other agency, but they came around and told us 'Make sure you don't have any animal parts on your table for sale.' I have turtle shells on my table because my business is called 'The Beaded Turtle.' I also have some pieces of badger and coyote fur that were given to the tribe by the people who made the movie *The New World*, but I use those just to display things on. I also have some turkey feathers on my table for display, and people say, 'How much are your turkey feathers?' I tell them they're not for sale. I'd get fined for that, and if I had any eagle, hawk, or owl feathers on my table for sale I'd probably get locked up for that. We can't use feathers from birds of prey like the hawk or owl."

At powwows she displays and sells her work. She usually has bracelets, barrettes, necklaces, bolos, and earrings on display. When she doesn't have any customers she's busy beading.

When she was little, they called her the "beadwork girl." She remembers that her maternal grandmother taught her beadworking when she was about nine or ten years old. She says, "I used to get teased because I loved doing beadwork so much I would rather stay inside and do that than play with the other kids. I started right off with seed beads, but at the Indian classes the young children started stringing pony or crow beads to make necklaces. When the older ones started working on the beading loom, it was kind of funny watching them try to pick the beads up with the needle; they would get so frustrated. I've been doing it so long that it's easy for me to pick them up, and I go so fast that I've had people ask me, 'Do you have a magnet on the end of that needle?' And I say, 'No, it's just years of doing it.'"

When Tammy started beading, her father made her a regular-sized loom, and then he made her a very wide one. She says, "He made me a necklace on a loom like the one he made me. We used fishing type nylon thread. It's really thick and strong. I have another piece we made that way, but we could never figure out a way to end it. Usually I run the thread back through the work until I get to a certain point, and then I cut the thread. If you just cut it off when you're through with the design the beads will fall off, so I either put beads on the ends, or I work the thread back through. But with that thick thread it's hard to run back through the beads, so I'm not sure how I'll finish it."

To some extent, the size of the loom determines the design. She has one loom that will hold 35 to 45 beads across, and she has another one that goes up to 120 spaces. To make a wider piece she beads strips and hooks them together. Usually her work is anywhere from 35 to 45 beads wide. She works out the background colors first and then the actual design. She then puts the design on beading graph paper indicating how many beads of one color go where. She feels the background is really important because that brings out the design. She uses a heavy nylon thread and draws it across a piece of beeswax to strengthen it and make it easier to thread the thin needle with its tiny hole. She says, "The beeswax strengthens the thread, and it makes the beadwork last a lot longer. Eventually those threads do rot. I have beadwork that my great grandmother made, and there are places where the thread is really, really frayed, and some beads are missing because there's no thread to hold them."

She thought about repairing her great grandmother's piece, but then she realized that the piece was a part of her great grandmother. She had held it and worked on it with her own hands, so it was part of Tammy's family history. She decided that, instead of changing the piece, she would either frame it or preserve it some other way.

Close-up of a beaded barrette with a turtle, the symbol of the Chickahominy Tribe, in the center.

Tammy helps Courtney with the beading on the loom.

Tammy also does beaded appliqué work. She sews the beads on a background fabric called Lacy's Stiff Stuff. Sometimes she makes a piece with a turtle that has a piece of wampum for his shell. When she does that she starts by using a little bit of glue to hold the wampum in place until she can get the beads around it. She says, "The very bottom layer of beads is a big bead, like a size 11, and then the second layer is size 11, and the next layer is size 15. I start out with the bigger beads, and then as I get closer to the top it kind of wraps itself around the wampum and holds it in place."

Her work is unique, and she was chosen to make the crowns for Little Miss Chickahominy and Junior Miss Chickahominy, young women who are chosen to represent the tribe. She made the crowns on Stiff Stuff. She drew the design on the fabric, and then beaded around that. She only uses the graph paper for designs done on the loom.

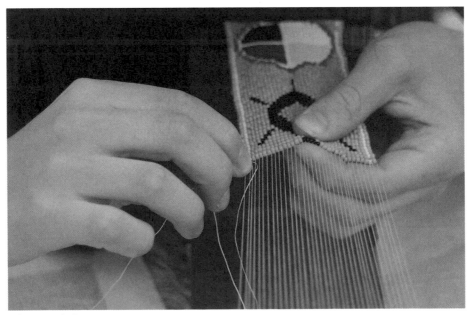

Close-up of above

Sometimes people see her work at a powwow and ask her to make something with special colors. She says, "Sometimes I don't think they're going to work, but they do."

The work she took to the last powwow took her six months to make because she cannot devote all her time to beadworking. She works at E.I. Dupont in Richmond so most days she can only do an hour of beadwork. "But," she says, "on my days off I do five or six hours of beading. It's like an obsession. I really do enjoy it. I am passionate about it. I just wish I could make a living at it. I'd like to teach beading, too. I've had so many children come to me and say, 'Can you teach me, can you teach me?' Even some adults have asked. They had done it when they were younger but haven't done it in a long time, like my sister, my brother and my sister-in-law. But I just can't fit it in with shift work. I don't have the time to teach them and to do my own beadwork."

Sometimes people bring her beaded things that they have bought elsewhere and ask her to fix them. Usually it's something that was not made by a Native American but rather in another country. "I can tell when something was made in Hong Kong, or Taiwan, because it not as strong as my work or other native's work. People bring me that stuff all the time to fix because it falls apart. It upsets my husband so much he says, 'You didn't even make that, why should you fix it?' They make pieces like that, and pass them off as Native American. I've seen pieces that say 'Made in Hong Kong,' or 'Made in Mexico' and they're very cheaply made. I can tell the difference just by looking at a piece. First of all, the beads are not glass, they're plastic-like, and I use all glass beads. Then the thread

Tammy at her booth, The Beaded Turtle, at a powwow.

they use is like regular sewing thread. It's not nylon, and I don't know if they're done on a machine or not. I don't know how they do that work, but I can tell what they are, and I know powwow organizers try not to allow that work at the powwows. They want all the work sold there to be Native American made."

She adds, "You can even tell the difference between Native made silver and turquoise jewelry. I did not realize that until we went to the opening of the Museum of the American Indian in Washington D.C. A display there showed the difference between Native American made and jewelry that had been made somewhere else. You could really see the difference. Some of the things they showed were exactly alike. Usually if something is handmade it might be very similar to another piece, but it's not going to be exactly the same. When you see something exactly like another piece you know that's machine done, or maybe not machine done, but with a mold. It's definitely not done by hand."

Even though Tammy makes some pieces that are similar to each other, they are never the same. She says, "Even if I make something the same as another piece, it's going to have a flaw in there somewhere. Sometimes I'm the only one that sees it, but it's there. I might have a blue bead where there should be a black bead. That's because the lighting wasn't right, or something, and the color looked the same to me. That's after hours and hours of beading. That's when I know I have to stop and put the work down. If I don't, my thread starts tangling up on me, and I start dropping beads. I know I've got to put it down for a while. That's the only thing that stops me."

Although she does not have time to teach many young people beading, she does work with her nieces Courtney and Taylor. Courtney sounds like she is getting as passionate about beading as her aunt. She says, "I think one of the reasons beading is so exciting is because it's limitless. There's so much room for creativity by creating your own designs. Plus if you combine it with the resources we have today – like the many different colored beads – there are just endless possibilities. I think that makes it a lot of fun, and it's a part of our heritage."

Tammy Jefferson in her traditional regalia wears the necklace her great uncle made. The necklace contains materials early Indians would have used before they started making adornments with trade beads obtained from the early settlers.

Chapter 3

Jessica Canaday
Chickahominy Indian, College Student, and Traditional Dancer

Braces and fancy manicured nails. Most young women are familiar with both. But because of stereotypes of the typical Indian woman, some are surprised to see Jessica Canaday, a Chickahominy Indian, wearing braces and manicured nails.

One might say Jessica lives in two different worlds. She works as a teller at a bank and attends Virginia Commonwealth University where she is studying to become a teacher. In other words, she is a contemporary young woman. However, she is also a young Indian woman who is proud of her heritage and participates in Indian events such as powwows.

Jessica Canaday in her regalia including a necklace she made on a beading loom.

A powwow is usually defined as a gathering of the people, a social event for Indian people. At one time they were private functions, but now many are open to the public. There is a dance circle which is usually blessed before the dancing begins, and drum groups provide the songs for the dancing. To some Indian people a powwow has more spiritual significance. They pause and

Jessica joins hands with two Grass Dancers in a Circle, or Friendship Dance at the VITAL powwow.

pray before they enter the dance circle, feeling that they are dancing to honor the Creator.

The regalia, or special clothing that Indians wear at powwows or special events, is an expression of who the person is and the type of dancing they do. Jessica is a traditional dancer. She wears the women's traditional regalia which consists of a buckskin dress, a shawl she carries over one arm, and a feather fan. Some traditional women dancers also wear a feather in their hair. Other women are fancy dancers and wear regalia made of satin, cotton or other colorful cloth that is often appliquéd with designs. The fancy dancers shawl has longer fringe and may also be appliquéd.

When Jessica is attending a powwow, people often want to take her picture. She remembers one time when she came out of the dance circle, and a woman asked her if she would pose for a picture with her son. Jessica says, "He took one look at me, and said, 'You're not an Indian.' I said, 'Yes I am.' Then he said, 'Indians don't wear braces.' I replied said, 'Yes they do if they want nice straight teeth.'"

Sometimes people confuse regalia with a costume, and when they wear their regalia for an occasion other than an Indian event, a person may draw strange comments. Courtney Wynn, Jessica's 14-year-old cousin, remembers one occasion where she wore her regalia in school and had an unpleasant experience. Courtney attends the Maggie Walker Governor's School for Government and International Studies in Richmond, Virginia. She wore her regalia because she was giving a persuasive speech on why Indians deserved federal recognition. She says, "After my speech was over I was going down to the locker room to change back into my regular clothes, and some seniors were in the senior commons area. They saw me walk by and they got really quiet, but when I got to the stairs they just burst out laughing. I kept going and changed, and when I was coming back up I went over to them and said, 'Were you guys laughing at me earlier when I walked by?' They said, "Well, were you the one in the Sacagawea costume?" I said, "First of all it's not a costume, it's called regalia, and I'm not pretending to be someone else, so it's definitely not a costume." And they said, 'Well, we're going to have to ask you to step out of the senior commons.'"

Courtney continues, "I said, 'I'm not going anywhere until you apologize for what you said.' They were kind of looking down and avoiding eye contact, and I told them 'I just want you all to know that that's not nice; that's very racist. It's not cool to laugh at people because of their heritage.' Then I just kind of walked away."

Jessica says she has also had problems at school with students making fun of her Native American heritage. She says, "I've had several incidents at school where people have made fun of me. When I was in middle school we put on a Native American program every year in November for Native American Month. I helped to head it up because I was really interested in sharing our cultural traditions with others, but when we put on our program some of the students

Jessica dances with Miss Chickahominy 2006, Carmen Wynn, and Junior Miss Chickahominy 2006, Ashton Montez at a VITAL powwow on the Chickahominy Tribal Grounds.

Tammy Jefferson completes Jessica's regalia with a beaded barrette that she made for her to wear after her reign as Miss Chickahominy when she had to turn in the crown.

laughed at us. They laughed at our regalia, and they laughed at us. It really bothered me. Last year when the organizers of our County Fair asked the Chickahominy Dancers to come and dance and asked me if I would participate, I was very reluctant to do it. I knew all of my previous classmates would be there. Even though I had graduated, we all pretty much live in the same area, and I knew they would be there. I remembered that earlier experience, and honestly I did not want to do it. My mom said I needed to. She said I needed to show them I wasn't afraid of them and their comments. I went, but it wasn't because I wanted to. Even in 2006 when people should know better they can be very cruel."

She adds, "My sister and brother have also had problems. My brother just recently had a very disturbing episode at school where somebody used a racial slur towards him, and he retaliated. Then he was the one suspended and not the person who made the slur. He was suspended for two days. My mom and dad tried to fight it with the principal, but things are as they are, and he was the one in trouble."

Jessica wants to be a teacher mainly because she loves children and wants to see them excel in life. Being a teacher would also give her opportunities to educate children about Native Americans. She says, "To have an opportunity to teach people about my Indian heritage would be an added bonus. Being a Native American, I could expose children at a young age to our culture. That might help do away with any stereotypes some develop because of a lack of information and lack of exposure to the Native American culture."

Recently, giving talks to school children has given Jessica the opportunity to share some information about her culture with young people. She began doing presentations with older members of her tribe but did the last program alone. She says, "The program was for students at Oak Knoll Middle School in Hanover County. I talked to 20 to 25 kids at a time and did eight sessions. It was a long day, but I enjoyed it. It was their Cultural Day, or Diversity Day, and they were studying other cultures. There were people there from Germany, Japan and Russia, and I represented the Native American culture. I brought some artifacts and showed them to the students. I brought dream catchers, pottery, my shawl, my fan, my turtle rattle, some bead work, tobacco and sweet grass. The sweet grass was given to me at the Upper Mattaponi powwow as head female dancer as a form of blessing. I was also given tobacco which is another traditional gift and form of blessing. Before they start a powwow, and even at practices they bless the drum with tobacco. Those students were very attentive, and I hope my talk helped erase some of the stereotypes they might have had."

Sometimes it is a little discouraging to realize how little students know about Indians in the area. Jessica says, "I've also worked with Bible School classes when they have a cultural fair, and the first thing I ask the children is if they have

Jessica at the 2006 VITAL powwow at the Chickahominy Tribal Grounds.

Jessica in the dance circle at a VITAL powwow for a Traditional Women's Dance.

Jessica, Miss Chickahominy 2003 with a
young dancer after an Intertribal Dance
at a Chickahominy powwow.

Jessica as Miss Chickahominy in 2003.

ever heard of the Chickahominy Tribe. Most of them haven't. And I ask them how many tribes in the state of Virginia are recognized by the state, and they have no idea. They are usually absolutely clueless. So I try to introduce the eight state recognized tribes to them and tell them where they are located. I also tell them how long the tribes have been established in those different locations. It is pretty amazing how many children have never heard of any of the tribes. I also tell them about powwows, a celebration of the Native people coming together and sharing their culture, and expressing their culture to others who want to learn more. I have found a few children who said they had heard of something like a powwow, and a few who had attended a powwow, but not many."

The Chickahominy Tribe is proud of young people like Jessica and chooses a Miss Chickahominy, a Junior Miss Chickahominy, and Little Miss Chickahominy. Jessica was chosen Miss Chickahominy in 2001, 2003, and 2004. She won the honor by being judged by a panel of three people. There were three sections to the contest: knowledge of the tribe, talent, and a question-and-answer segment. Jessica says, "We had to wear our regalia and show our Native American voice."

As Miss Chickahominy she represented her tribe at several powwows and events. She has also been honored by being asked to be head female dancer at several powwows. She was first head female dancer at the first annual VITAL

(Virginia Indian Tribal Alliance for Life) powwow. She says, "The theme for that was enriching the lives of the youth, trying to encourage the youth to gain awareness and show interest in their culture. Then I was asked to be head female dancer at the Upper Mattaponi powwow and last year for ours. Next year I've been asked to be head female dancer for the Piscataway powwow in Maryland. I'm very excited about that. It will be quite an honor as it's going to be their 50th anniversary powwow, a very special one."

Jessica explains, "There are always two lead dancers: a female and a male. As part of the female's duties, she leads the women dancers during intertribal dances. When I am lead dancer, no one can start dancing until I do, and then they are supposed to follow me and the way I dance. Since I'm a traditional dancer, when the time comes for the women's traditional exhibition, and we go into the circle, the ladies can't start dancing until I do. The head or lead dancers are required to dance every dance except the exhibition dances. I wouldn't dance a woman's Fancy Dance, or a men's Grass Dance, but I have to dance all the intertribal, circle dances, and any honor dances. The Two Step is the only dance where Indian men and women dance together, and everyone has to follow the steps that the lead dancers do. We choose all the steps ourselves. We can weave in and out, join hands and dance, or do something like the Virginia Reel – whatever we do they have to do too."

Jessica says that the type of dancing she does is what she's learned in her tribe over the years from her people. Her Aunt Rhonda Canaday began teaching her dances when she was five or six. She says, "My mom has never danced with me in the circle, but she has always attended the powwows with me, and she's always made my regalia. I had my first regalia when I was two, and I remember it because of pictures my parents have of me in it. My sister and I would go into the circle with my Aunt Rhonda. I've learned all my steps from her. I followed her feet and did what she did. She's been a head female dancer several times, so she's quite a good dancer. I credit her with teaching me to dance well enough to be asked to be a head dancer today."

She continues, "I love to dance, and I love being with so many people I care about. Most of the time when I'm dancing I'm having fun, because so many of the people are my friends. When I'm in that setting in the dance circle with them it just makes me feel so good, because they share the same love and passion for our culture that I do. I'm so very proud to be out there with them."

One fall instead of regalia she wore a red velvet dress when representing a part of Indian history. She was chosen to play the part of Pocahontas, or Lady Rebecca as she was known after her conversion to Christianity, at the recreation of the wedding of Pocahontas and John Rolfe. The recreation was held at Henricus Historical Park although the actual wedding was in Jamestown.

Jessica portraying Pocahontas or Lady Rebecca in a recreation of her marriage to John Rolfe reenacted at Henricus Historical Park. The actual wedding took place at Jamestown.

Jessica's Indian name, "Adoring Eyes," was given to her at the age of 15 by her Aunt Arnette Adkins. Jessica remembers that it was the summer before she was crowned Miss Chickahominy 2001. Some children are given an Indian name at birth, and it is on their birth certificates. Others are given their Indian names at different ages by medicine men at various powwows or by a family member later in life. Some names are chosen because a child shows special traits or interests. Jessica says, "My mom said she didn't want to give us an Indian name at birth because she wanted it to be our decision to be a member of the tribe. You can only be a member of the tribe when you turn 16. When I turned 16, she didn't really ask me; she just said 'When are you going to join?' It was just understood that we would all be members, and we all are. I have one brother who is 17, and an 18-year-old sister. They're both members of the tribe, too."

Jessica is not only proud of her heritage, she is proud of her family. She says, "I work, I go to school, and I absolutely love my family. I would not trade them for anything in this world. And I believe family is why I'm here today. It's my foundation for life. We're such a tightly knit community down here in Charles City that if I don't want what my mom has fixed for dinner, I can just go next door to my grandmother's house, and she will fix me whatever I want. After I eat there I can drive three minutes down the road to my other grandmother's house for dessert. I'm so blessed to have all of my grandparents healthy and alive. I have such a good relationship with all four of them. I think of members of the Chickahominy tribe as members of my family too. We hardly ever call anyone Mr. or Mrs. down here; everyone is Aunt or Uncle, or some other type of endearment. We're extremely close down here, and I wouldn't trade that for anything."

The only thing that seems to be missing for Jessica and other tribal members is federal recognition. It's hard to believe that the Indians that met the English back in 1607 are not recognized by the federal government. The state-recognized tribes of Virginia predate the United States and had treaties with the English who settled the land, but after 400 years do not have federal recognition. Jessica feels it is important to get federal recognition for her family, especially her grandparents for health care and other benefits. She says, "I think they deserve it because if it wasn't for them I wouldn't be here today. They have paved such a wonderful path for me. They had to struggle so hard when they were going through the Walter Plecker days and his documentary genocide attempts. To hear what they went through every day is difficult. My dad was born at home, so his birth certificate indicates that he is Native American. But his younger brother who was born in the hospital has "white" marked on his birth certificate, and so does my mom. It really hurts to be denied your Native American identity. They struggled so much to retain their heritage, they deserve federal recognition.

They need to see federal recognition before they pass on. Plus, federal recognition will also help the children of this tribe. I was denied so many scholarships because we are not federally recognized. There was a web site where you could put in your profile, and based on that it would look up all the scholarships that applied to you. I had tons upon tons of scholarships that fit my profile because I put in Native America, but the criteria for the larger scholarships said you had to be from a federally recognized tribe. I did receive a small scholarship for Virginia Indians called the Heather Dayton Memorial Scholarship, and my sister was awarded it this year at her graduation. But being federally recognized would open so many doors for the young people who apply for scholarship and grant money. I'm fortunate my parents could help me with school."

Chapter 4

✳

Judith "Tacanomeika" Fortune
Rappahannock Dance Coordinator

The five Rappahannock women stand tall and proud as they wait to enter the dance circle at the Rappahannock Tribal Grounds. As the drummers start, they enter the circle and begin their Shawl Dance.

Judith Fortune, Dance Coordinator for the tribe, whose Indian name means "Keeper of the Children," says that the dance group fluctuates. There are usually around ten dancers and drummers. They don't hold regular practices because everyone knows all the dances, but sometimes when they have a dance presentation scheduled, they get together and go over the dances that they are going to perform. In the summer, they show the young children how to do the specialty dances, or intertribal dances, that they might not have learned how to do by then.

Judith learned many of the Rappahannock dances when she was a child. She remembers that Saturdays were usually social occasions when members of the tribe would get together. She says, "Our parents would say, 'OK you guys come over here, and we're going to show you how to do this.'"

One particular dance was passed down from mother to daughter. The Squaw Dance was one of the first dances the girls learned. It was a type of introductory dance. It didn't have a specific meaning that she can recall; it was just a mother - daughter dance where the women taught the girls how to move their feet. Judith says, "I haven't done that for years, ever since my mom taught it to me. It's not really something that we do now."

Many tribes may have the same name for a particular dance such as the Green Corn Dance, the Shawl Dance, and the Canoe Dance. The Rappahannocks have their own traditional way of dancing these dances. Dances such as the Deer Hunter Dance and Welcome Dance are also old dances passed down from older generations. All of these dances are called "specialty dances." Other dances that everyone does at powwows are called intertribal dances. Most of the adults know how to do intertribal dances like the Men's Traditional Dance, the Women's Traditional Dance, or the Two Step.

Some specialty dances the Rappahannocks do, like the Shawl Dance, are different from the specialty dances that other dancers do. Judith says, "Our Shawl Dance is a social dance among the Rappahannock women. It symbolizes the free spirit of the women. As they dance and hold out their shawls it seems as if their arms are wings, and their movements are like a butterfly or a bird flowing with the wind. It's not the same as a Fancy Dancer's Shawl Dance which incorporates a lot of spins and twirls and varied footwork. A Fancy Dancer has different regalia from what we wear as Traditional Dancers, so it looks a lot different from our dance."

Each tribe may have different thoughts and ideas on their dances or on how their dances are interpreted. You may see a similar dance at a powwow and someone will say, "This dance has a story, and this is what it means." Judith explains, "It may be their story, but it might not necessarily be our story. We did a presentation once, and after we explained and did one of our dances, someone said, 'Well, that's not right, that's not what it means, and that's not the way to do it,' and I said, 'That's not how you do it, but that's how we do it.'"

L to R. Drummers Jacob Fortune-Deuber and Clarence Seay, and dancers Barbara "Desert Flower" Williams and Joan "Little Swan" Johnson listen to Judith Fortune (between the drummers) discuss a song for their run through of the Shawl Dance.

She adds, "I find it educational to watch how other tribes do their dances. I haven't seen any other tribe do the Welcome Dance exactly like we do it. There are different variations of it. We do two types of welcome dances, a contemporary Welcome Dance and then our traditional Welcome Dance. In the traditional Welcome Dance the dancers form a circle, and one main dancer, or host dancer, starts in the center of the circle. That dancer holds a dancing stick. Usually when you have a Welcome Dance you have a representative from each tribe, and the host person, or the leader, holds the stick and approaches someone, and asks them to accept the dancing stick and dance in the circle. Then they pass it to someone else and invite them to dance. That is our traditional one. In the contemporary one the men and women dance together, and they do a ruffling of their feathers – the fans. It's a very graceful dance. We don't normally do our traditional Welcome Dance at a powwow because not all the dancers that come would know how to do that particular dance."

The Welcome Dance involves both men and women, but usually the dances are for one or the other. One of the Rappahannock dances that men do is the Deer Hunter Dance. Judith describes the dance this way, "Depending on the size of the dance group, one, or possibly two dancers, portray a deer, and the other men are the hunters. They dance around mimicking the moves of a hunter. Of course the dancers always have to listen to the drum beat because they dance according to the drum. The drummers don't beat according to the dancers, and they control how long or short a dance might be. The dancers take their cue from the drum. In the Deer Hunter Dance, the dancers are dancing around the deer as it grazes. All of a sudden the drum beat picks up signifying that the hunter sees the deer, and the deer sees him. Then they dance back and forth in rapid movements. Next there's a very strong beat representing the arrow shooting into the deer. After the deer has fallen, the hunters dance around slowly, and they raise their weapons up to the sky. They give the Great

L to R. Jacob Fortune-Deuber, Judith Fortune, and Clarence Seay discuss a song for a run through of the Rappahannock Shawl Dance.

L to R Barbara Williams, Judith Fortune, Faye Fortune, and Joan Johnson mimic the motions of planting corn as they run through the Rappahannock Green Corn Dance.

L to R Faye Fortune and her sister Judith Fortune execute one of the movements in the Rappahannock Green Corn Dance.

L to R Faye Fortune, Joan Johnson, Barbara Williams, and Judith Fortune some of the members of the Rappahannock Tribal Dancers hold bowls high to give thanks to the Great Spirit for providing corn for food, and ask His blessings for a bountiful harvest in the Rappahannock Green Corn Dance.

Spirit thanks for the food that he's provided to them to take back to their village. In this particular dance they also give thanks to their brother the deer for his life so that they could live."

Judith adds, "One of the dances that we frequently do if we are doing a presentation, or program, is the Green Corn Dance. That is a women's dance. The women make motions as if they are planting corn in the four directions, north, south, east, and west. They come together in the middle of the circle and raise their arms to the sky and point to the four directions. That is done five times for the five seasons - spring, summer, the green corn season, fall, and winter. In the spring the corn is planted. In that season it is reproducing, or bringing about new life. Summer is the growing season. Then there is a season between summer and fall, which we call the green corn harvest season. That is when the corn is harvested for consumption. Then in the fall the remainder of the corn is harvested and stored away for the winter season. At the end of the dance, each dancer raises a bowl up to thank the Great Spirit for the food he's providing and at the same time to ask his blessing for a good crop.

Some of the more contemporary dances have been incorporated in later years. Dancers learned them from going to powwows and seeing other dancers and dances. There are common dances that many of the Virginia tribes know and have adopted.

The Traditional Women's Dance, Traditional Men's Dance, the Circle Dance, (sometimes called the Friendship Dance), and the Two Step are all dances that one will see at most powwows, and most tribes do them in a similar manner.

The drummers sing or chant while they drum. As Judith says, "Some sing words, and others have chants with them, but usually we call them songs." At a powwow the master of ceremonies will announce each dance and ask the drum for an appropriate song for that dance. There are some dances that are done at powwows that are not indigenous to our state. We don't have the Jingle Dance. You will recognize its dancer by her regalia. Over 300 metal shaped cones originally made from chewing tobacco can lids are sewn in several rows around the dress. As the dancer moves, they jingle and create a musical sound. She says, "That dance did not originate here, but it's a beautiful dance. One of the little girls in our tribe wants to be a Jingle Dancer, so we wouldn't deny her that, if that's what she feels she wants to do, but it's not an indigenous dance for the Rappahannocks."

The Rappahannock Dancers have been invited to various places. Some have been in Virginia and some in other parts of the world.

Judith says, "We used to go to George Washington's Birthplace in Westmoreland County for a special program, and we really enjoyed going there. In certain places you feel more of an energy, and we always felt like there was a lot of energy there. It was right beside the water in a wooded area, and there were

L to R. Judith Fortune, Barbara Williams, Joan Johnson, and Faye Fortune run through the Rappahannock Shawl Dance in the dance circle at the Rappahannock Tribal Grounds.

always eagles flying above while we danced. The Park Ranger said he felt that the eagles were more abundant when we were there."

They have also been to Europe. In 1988 they went to France for the Rio De La Cote d' Jour Festival. It was a carnival held in Nice, France. At that event there were dancers from Maryland, North Carolina, and Virginia. She says, "It was quite an experience. It was exciting to be around the other Native people and meet Indians from North Carolina. We already knew some of the people from Maryland, so it was nice to see them, too. In addition to Native Americans, they had people from other countries who were also there for the festival. It was a way of celebrating different cultures. The French people were very generous and kind. We had a lovely time, and went sightseeing when we weren't performing."

Judith Fortune, in front, and her sister Faye Fort-une hold their arms out to echo the movements of a butterfly or bird in the Rappahannock Shawl Dance.

Some of the Rappahannock Dancers and Drummers also participated in the trip to England during the 2007 observance of the 400th anniversary of the establishment of the first permanent English colony in the New World at Jamestown. That trip included members from each of the eight state-recognized tribes in Virginia. Leaders of the tribes, as well as potters and other craft people, made the trip as well as drummers and dancers. They went to Kent County where Pocahontas is buried, and in addition to presentations to the general public, they visited schools. There they talked to students and demonstrated Virginia Indian cultural traditions.

Among Native Americans, dance combines many aspects of their culture. It has its social aspects, but it also has spiritual aspects. The dances reflect their respect for each other and the Great Spirit. During the Women's Traditional Dance many of the men stand around the outside of the circle and hold their feather fans high to show their respect for the women. Women often do the same when the Traditional Male dancers dance.

At most powwows the dance circle is blessed before the dancing begins, and outsiders are not allowed to enter the dance circle unless they are invited. But there are also dances like the Friendship Dance, or Circle Dance, where everyone is invited to dance, and dancing together can be an integral part of learning about others and sharing cultural traditions.

Faye Fortune and the Rappahannock Dancers perform their Shawl Dance at a powwow.

Judith Fortune dancing at a Rappahannock powwow.

For the young people, especially the young men who are drummers, it is difficult to keep their regalia up because they grow so quickly. Judith says, "We were supposed to be going somewhere, and we said, 'Let's get your regalias out and replenish them and make sure everything's together.' Then my nephew put his on, and he'd grown so much it didn't fit. The leather that we use in the regalias can get very expensive, so a lot of times we'll pass regalia down to a younger person that it fits. What we had to do on my nephew's leggings was add pieces of deer skin to extend the length. But you can only do that for a certain period of time. For the trip to England he had to have new leggings made because he had completely outgrown his old ones."

Judith says, "My regalia is a traditional cloth, woman's regalia. My first regalia was buckskin, and then I had an elk skin. But it's so warm in the summer that I chose to make it lighter, and I used cloth. I did the beading on the front of it. It has a yellow flower on the front because I love yellow. To me it represents sunshine, brightness, happiness, and life."

All of Judith's brothers and sisters are active in the tribe. "Mother had four boys and four girls, and all of us dance or drum. We strive very hard in today's society to motivate our young people and keep their spirits interested in their culture. Because they go to public schools, they are involved in a lot of activities. We tell them, 'Even though you're living in a modern world, we also want you to maintain and preserve your heritage and your culture.' But it's difficult for them, sometimes playing softball or baseball one weekend and dancing at a powwow in their regalia the next weekend. They're like busy beavers, and that's appropriate because the symbol for our tribe is the beaver."

Chapter 5

※

Voncie "Bright Eyes" Fortune
Rappahannock Cornhusk Basket Maker and Potter

When most people get fresh corn, they shuck it, cook the corn, and throw away the shucks, but not Voncie Fortune. This member of the Rappahannock tribe dries the shucks and uses them to make cornhusk baskets.

She says, "I learned how to make baskets out of cornhusks a long time ago. I used to watch my aunt and uncle make them. Also, my aunt had a book that showed traditional Native American crafts, and that type of basket was in there. When I made the bottom of my first basket, it looked just like the picture in the book. That first basket didn't turn out too bad."

Voncie and her daughter, Vanessa Schoch, work on a cornhusk basket.

Voncie dips the cornhusks into water to make them pliable before starting to work on a row for a cornhusk basket.

Voncie and her granddaughter, Shelby Seay, at work.

Voncie shows her 14-year-old granddaughter, Shelby Seay, how to sew a point on a row for a basket.

Voncie adding to a row for a cornhusk basket.

Adding the last row to a basket.

The early baskets were made with tools made from natural materials, but with the introduction of metal needles after the settlers arrived at Jamestown, the methods of making them probably changed. By the time Voncie began making cornhusk baskets, metal needles were used.

Making a cornhusk basket is not an easy process, and it takes Voncie about a week to finish one. She starts by slitting bar grass, which is a large plant that grows wild. She does this to make the thread that she uses to sew the basket together. Then she starts with the bottom of the basket. She dips the husk in water

Voncie and her daughter, Vanessa Schoch, with a finished cornhusk basket.

to make it more pliable. She twists the husk, coils it around, and sews the coils together. As she says, "You carry it around and around and sew them together. You continue to go around and sew until it's the size you want. You join the pieces together by leaving one of the ends open enough to put one piece inside the other and then twist it. The bottom is really the hardest part of making the basket."

The body of the basket has rows of cornhusks that have little points on them. The husk is cut to size with scissors, then wet, and folded until it is about as wide as her finger. Then she folds the husk and twists it to make a little peak on it. As she builds the sides of the basket up, she sews through the folded husk, a difficult task that is hard on the fingers. Sometimes she uses the table she is working on to help push the needle through the husks. Once the body of the basket is the size she wants it, she adds a handle and lines the inside with a soft flannel or felt-like material.

The baskets can be very useful. When her aunt kept chickens, she used them to collect eggs. She also remembers a time when she was quite young when she was working on a basket, and Dr. Frank Speck came to visit. He saw what she was making and asked if he could have one. She says, "I gave him a basket and he put a dozen eggs in it and carried it back to Philadelphia and not one broke."

Dr. Speck was the chairman of the Department of Anthropology at the University of Pennsylvania. He was an American ethnologist who specialized in the cultures of the Eastern Woodland Indians. He regularly stayed with the Indians he studied and collected all aspects of their culture.

Voncie remembers, "I was about 10 or 12 years old when Dr. Speck visited our tribe. He came down several times and sometimes brought his family or students with him. He usually stayed a couple of weeks. He stayed with my Aunt Susie, and his daughter stayed at my house. His daughter and I were about the same age, and he would take us on walks through the woods. Little green snakes would sometime hang from the trees, and he would laugh at us cause we would start hollering when a snake fell on our heads. But the worst was a big black snake. There was a stump behind our house, and there was a big black snake in that stump. Dr. Speck used to go down there, and he would do or say something, and that snake would come out of the stump. It was the biggest snake I've ever seen. He would stand there and hold his hands apart and make his daughter get at one end and me at the other end so that he could stretch it out. That snake was just as cold as ice. I don't know why he wanted us to do that unless he wanted to show us that the snake wouldn't bite us. Now that was one thing I didn't like to do when he came.

He was a great man, however, who was always looking for something. He'd come every day and we'd walk all over the place. We'd find pieces of pottery and sometimes arrows. We didn't always find much, but when we found something he always wanted to show us what it was and talk about it. Sometimes he brought students with him, and they stayed at my mom's house. They would watch us to see what we did, and how we did it. He liked to watch my mom cook. The students would also get up in the morning to watch mom feed her chickens. All the time they were watching everything she did and how she did it. Then he would write it up. I gave him a basket, and he gave me things, too. I have a piece of pottery he gave me, and some little pouches."

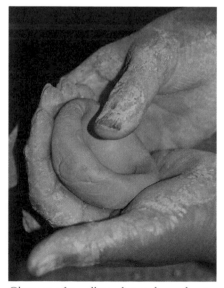

Close up of small pinch pot she makes to begin a pot.

Dr. Speck wrote several articles about the Eastern Woodland Indians including one about the Rappahannocks entitled "Rappahannock Taking Devices – Traps, Hunting and Fishing." He got some of the material for that article from Voncie's father.

She says, "My dad used to make traps for catching birds and rabbits. He also showed the boys how to fix a trap to catch a deer. He bent a little sapling over, and as much as I can remember, he put something near there, and when the deer bent over to pick up what was there, it would step on something that would trigger the trap, and it'd get caught. He used to set them up to show us how the older people caught deer."

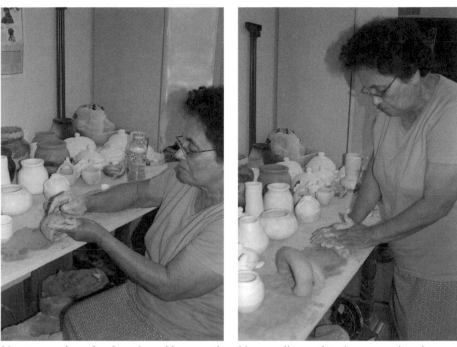

Voncie smoothing the clay after adding a coil.   *Voncie rolls a coil to form an arch to begin making a pot.*

Voncie adds, "When we were small we wanted to hunt like the adults did, but we weren't quite old enough to hunt deer, so we used to catch snow birds, those little birds you only see in the winter. Adults caught them too, but it was easy hunting for the children. We would get a board – anything that would hold the birds down. We'd set the board up and tie a piece of string to it. Then we'd put meal around so the birds would come to eat. We'd watch, and when they came around to eat the meal we'd pull the string, and that would make the board fall on them. We'd pick the feathers off, clean them, get a string and tie it to their feet, and hang them up by the fireplace. That fire would be hot enough to fry those little birds. They were really small. It was hardly worth picking the meat off them, as it was only about as much as the end of your thumb."

When she was young, Voncie remembers that she was always trying to do the things she saw the older people doing. She says, "My mom made pottery. I guess just seeing her do it a couple of times made me want to see if I could do it too. There was a stream right in back of my home, and there was clay there. I told my mom, 'I'm going to make a pot.' And she said, 'Well, go ahead and try.' I made some pieces of pottery, and at that time we didn't have a kiln, so I put them in our wood cook stove and baked them just like we baked bread."

When Voncie made a head of an Indian, she baked the head in the wood stove. Now she uses a kiln in the Rappahannock Tribal Center to bisque fire her

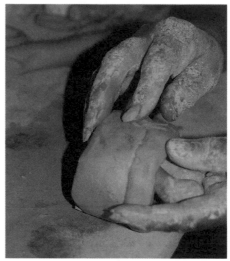

Close up of adding a coil to the clay pot.   *Close up of left.*

pottery before she "burns" or fires it outdoors. Historically, Powhatan Indians dug a pit and then put the hardened clay pieces into it and put sticks and pine tags over them. They set fire to the sticks, and the pottery got fired, or burned, that way. Sometime later some Indians began burning pottery with cow manure. Voncie said she tried using dried cow manure once or twice after the pieces had been bisqued for the burning phase. She said that made a little more smoke which gave the pots clouds of darker colors, but that they really didn't look that different. Then her family got rid of their cows, so now she just uses pine tags, green pine needles, little sticks, and anything that smothers the fire so that it smokes. Like potters from other tribes, she covers the fire with something metal to keep the smoke in while the pots are being burned.

Voncie's daughter Judith has also made some pottery, and another daughter, Faye, is starting to learn. Faye remembers, "We used to get clay from different places. Some would be gray, and from other river banks it would be reddish. We also got clay from the banks of Accapataugh Beach, but a private owner purchased the land and the clay was no longer accessible. Accapataugh Beach was one of the locations of a Rappahannock King's town, when Chief Accapataugh ruled. In 1658 the great men of the Rappahannocks signed a peace treaty with Colonel Moore Fauntleroy on behalf of King Accapataugh although he was deceased. Their king had requested that his friend Colonel Fauntleroy be allowed to live on his land in peace."

"That clay was better than this commercial clay I have to use now," Voncie says. "It felt like it was smoother. With this commercial clay you have to put a lot of water with it to make it soft. The other probably held some of the water from the river because it came from the banks. Now I buy a bag of gray clay which turns white when it's fired, and a bag of brownish or reddish clay."

She starts her pottery by mashing the clay together on a hard surface. If it is not smooth and all together, it will crack. She begins her ceramic pieces a little differently than most traditional potters. She rolls out a very thick coil and then sets it up like an arch, which she leaves overnight. She starts making the pot the next day. After that most of the work of making a coil pot is similar to what other Indian potters do. She breaks off a piece of clay and rolls it in her hand to form a ball. Then she puts her finger in the ball and works it around and around to make a little pinch pot. Next she takes some more of the thick coil and rolls it into another coil. As she adds coils, she usually scores the edge of the pot before she puts the new coil on to make a tight seal.

Voncie explains, "After I add a coil, I have to smooth the inside and smooth the outside. You can't do it fast. You have to take your time. After I've added a few coils, I start shaping it. I use a paddle and hit the clay with the paddle. I've got to smack it around a little bit. Sometimes when I'm making a pot, I get it half way done and don't like it. Then I tear it all to pieces, and start again. When I get the pot about five inches tall, I have to let it dry a little bit. If it's soft it won't stand up enough for me to put another coil on. I say it sits down. So I let it dry overnight. I take a piece of paper and wet the paper and put it down inside the pot. Then I'll take a rag or something and put it over the top of it; that will stop it from getting too dry. The next day I can score the top and start adding more coils.

These pots are just for decoration, but in the old days they would add broken, or ground up eggs shells or oyster shells to the clay, and they could cook in the pots. I made a great big one that is about two feet tall. We cooked in that at a powwow. We were testing it, and it worked," she adds.

Voncie also makes boxes, some in the shape of a turtle. The area that is the

Voncie takes the top off a clay turtle box.   *One of Voncie's clay turtle boxes.*

shell lifts off. When Chief Richardson visited the White House, she took one of Voncie's turtle boxes and gave it to President Bush. Voncie says, "A lot of people ask me why I make turtles because our symbol is the beaver, but I was just sitting here one day, and it came to me, 'Why don't you make a turtle?' So I started making the turtles, and everybody who came to our powwow wanted the turtles, so I kept making them. I have one lady who comes to our powwow every year and buys six of them. They're very popular, I guess, because they're so different."

Something else that she does that is a little unusual is combine the reddish clay with the gray clay so that when it is fired there are areas of red on the pot. She usually

doesn't burn those; she burnishes them with a wooden tool or the back of a spoon to make them shiny. She also burns some of the ones made out of the reddish clay and gets dark or black clouds on the red background.

Like her mother and father before her, Voncie occasionally tells her children about the old ways and shows them how to make pottery or cornhusk baskets, but her daughter, Judy, would like her to write some of her memories and experiences down so that they can be carried on to future generations.

Two pots with "clouds" (dark areas) that have been burned.

A table full of Voncie's pottery. The ones with the dark areas have been burned; the others are ready to be burned.

Voncie combined gray and red clay to make this pot.

Chapter 6

Mildred "Pale Moon" Moore
Pamunkey Potter

The old schoolhouse on the Pamunkey Reservation stands empty now. The little white one-room building's windows are boarded up, and the steps are not very safe. But the blackboard is still in place, as is the round stove that burned wood and coal in the winter to keep the eight children and their teacher warm.

Mildred Moore remembers going to school there when grades one through eight were taught by one teacher in the little building. She also remembers the paddle the teacher used to enforce discipline. Mildred says, "She was famous for that. We didn't do anything real bad, maybe throw a spitball or something, but she would whack one of us with that paddle and send us to stand in the cloak room just about every day. I got whacked plenty of times and spent my share of time in the cloak room."

The teacher also had a bell that she would ring to call the children in from recess. "I don't know what happened to that bell. I left the reservation when I got married, and I moved back here when my mother got sick. By that time the school was closed, because the schools had been integrated, and children were going to school in West Point. We got the bell from the old school, and my mother used to ring the bell if she needed help. A few years ago I loaned it to someone, and they loaned it to someone else, and now no one knows where it is."

As a child, Mildred always looked forward to the end of the school day so she could cross the yard to the Pottery School that was behind the school. The Pottery School was started by the state during the Depression to help members of the tribe make money by selling their pottery to tourists. At that time a train stopped at the reservation, and people came there to buy pottery or ceramics. The pottery was made using the traditional hand coiled method, and each piece took a long time to make.

The state gave the tribe the materials to build the Pottery School and sent a teacher to help the Pamunkey learn new and easier methods of making pieces with clay. Not only did it take a long time to make a coil pot, but firing the pieces in pits dug in the ground was not a dependable method of finishing the ceramic pieces. The weather could affect the process. If it was too cold when the hot pieces were taken out

of the pit, they would crack or break, so the teacher sent by the state introduced the Indians to the kiln. The wood burning kiln was an easier and safer way to fire the pottery. But when the pieces were fired they were a plain brown and not very attractive, so he showed them how to apply glaze and colorful decorations and pictographs to the pottery. Another teacher taught them to use molds as that speeded up the process even more.

By the time Mildred started going there, the state had stopped sending a teacher, and some of the women had gone back to making hand-built pottery. Others still used molds that were stored in a little room in the back on shelves according

Mildred keeps the clay dug from the Pamunkey River bank in a bucket of water and stirs it until it is the right consistency with which to work.

to subject matter. Molds for pitchers were in one place, and those for vases were in another. Most of the molds were plaster of Paris and had been formed from an original clay piece that someone had made. The molds belonged to the individual women and were sold or passed down to family members if someone died.

Mildred has a special hump mold for a frog plate that has been passed down to her. She rolls clay with a rolling pin until it is the correct thickness and then places it over the mold. She presses the clay down and cuts off the excess around the edges. As she works she watches for air bubbles in the clay. If she sees one she pops it with a knife. If there are any air bubbles left in the clay, it will explode when it is fired. She smoothes the clay

Mildred and the large pot she made using the coil method of construction.

photo by Teresa Koren, The Valentine Richmond History Center

Mildred holds a small coil pot she made during a demonstration at The Valentine Richmond's History Center.

Three coil pots by Gentle Rain (Mildred).

off and leaves it on the mold to dry. After it has dried and been fired once, she decorates the frog with whatever colors suit her fancy.

Other pieces made with molds are decorated with pictographs. As previously mentioned, the pictographs originated when the pottery school had a teacher. Mildred is not sure whether the teacher showed them pictures of Indian pottery made in the west that was decorated with designs and pictographs, or whether he just told them that they could decorate their pottery that way. However they evolved, people will not see pictographs used quite the way they are used on Pamunkey Pottery School work.

There are three stories that are told on the pottery. The symbol in the center may not be the same on each piece, and the edge may be decorated differently, but the pictographs that circle the piece tell either the story of Pocahontas and John Smith, the terms of the Treaty of 1646, or how meat was dried and preserved. Mildred says she doesn't remember the story or symbols used for the one about meat, but the Pocahontas plate is very popular. Some of the symbols are easy to figure out – a stick figure with a feather in the back of the head was an Indian – men with rifles were white men – and an upside down man indicated a man that had been killed. But others are not so obvious. A diamond with another diamond inside it means "good luck," and two crossed arrows means "no harm." So when one reads the pictographs on the Pocahontas plate, its 16 symbols mean, "Indians while hunting discover white man standing in shallow water. Indians agree to kill white man at chief's seat. Indian maiden disagrees with Indian men (and) makes no harm for white man but good wishes."

Mildred enjoyed her time in the Pottery School. "I'd spend an hour or so there. My grandfather's brother's wife taught me how to make some small things like Indian canoes and little animals with the clay. She was very old and the only one who took the time to work with me. The other women were too busy; they couldn't be bothered with me. But she would say, 'Mildred come here and sit beside me, and I'll teach you everything I know.'"

At one time there were five or six women who worked at the two long tables there, and sometimes they would sing as they worked. Mildred doesn't remember the words to the songs, but she knows that they had some they made up themselves. Some day she hopes to go through some of the boxes of material that were packed up after the pottery school building had deteriorated to the point that it wasn't safe to be used. She would like to find those songs as well as the records of the Pottery Guild. The women who made pottery formed a guild and went to different locations to sell their work.

Making pottery on the reservation began long before the Pottery School was created. Pamunkey Indians had been making hand built pottery with clay from the banks of the Pamunkey River since before the colonists settled Jamestown. The tribe is unique because it is one of only a few tribes east of the Mississippi who have been making pottery continuously since aboriginal times.

Mildred remembers, "The day the people dug clay from the riverbank used to be a big day. There was one special hole down there, and its location was kept secret. Only the men who dug the clay and some of the women knew where it was. Everyone would go down to the river, and it was like a celebration. There was a ceremony, and people used to bring food and things for the day of digging. But that stopped years ago, and now we either have to dig clay ourselves or get someone to dig it for us."

After the clay is dug it has to be prepared for making pottery. First it is allowed to dry out and then crushed into pieces with rocks. The crushed clay is

Mildred trims the excess clay from the edges of the frog on the hump mold.

Mildred lifts a piece of clay she has rolled out to place on the frog mold.

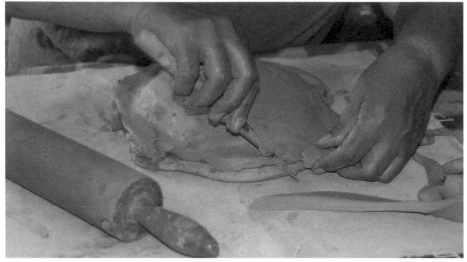

Close up of Mildred trimming the excess clay from the edges of the frog on the hump mold.

put in water and left until it gets soupy. It is stirred every so often, and then strained through a screen to get all the stones and little twigs out. After that it is put back into another bucket and sits until the water comes to the top. Then the water is poured off, and the clay sits some more. This process can take several days. Each day the water is poured off until the clay is the consistency of heavy cream. Finally the clay is poured onto plaster slabs called bats. The plaster draws the water out, and the clay stays on the bats until it sticks together and can be lifted off. As Mildred says,

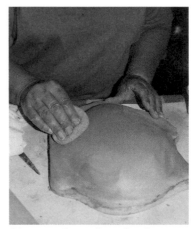

Close up of smoothing the clay on the mold.

"That's how you know you can work the clay – when it sticks together. Then you can put it in plastic or buckets, or whatever you want to use to store it, and you use it as you need it."

Mildred still prepares her clay that way and uses it either to make pieces on the hump mold or by hand. For the molds of bowls or other shaped pieces the clay is left in a liquid state and poured into the mold.

Historically most of the pieces were made by hand, and pots and bowls were made using the coil method of construction. Mildred also makes pieces using that method of construction. The traditional coil pieces are also called black ware because once they are fired, the outside of the piece is black. It can be decorated with designs that are etched into the clay in the leather hard stage.

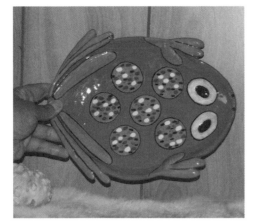

A finished frog plate.

A plate Mildred decorated with the story of Pocahontas and John Smith

To begin a coil pot Mildred uses a little plaster bowl called a puki to hold the base and stabilize the pot as it is built. Most of the pots are five or six inches high. But once Mildred made a pot that was three feet tall. She says, "I didn't set out to make a pot that big, but I just kept building and building and building to see how far I could go before it started toppling over. I worked on it for about four months and wrapped it in plastic each time I stopped working on it. It finally did start to topple, and I thought it looked good at that point, so I stopped. Then I didn't know how I was going to fire it. There was nothing big enough to hold it, so I dug a hole and laid it on its side and burned it down there. It stood here for years, and I never knew why I did it, but now I know – because it's a showpiece. Everybody is amazed when they see something this big done all by hand."

Mildred likes to work in a quiet room. She clears her kitchen table, and gets out the clay she has been keeping moist wrapped in plastic. As she begins to work, she places her puki to the side of the table, pounding the clay on the table to get all the air bubbles out. As she works with the clay, the only sounds you can hear are the occasional chirping of birds outside the window. She says, "I like it quiet when I work. No radio, no TV. I don't want any distractions. Actually working with clay is relaxing and very therapeutic. Once you get a feel for the clay, it becomes your best friend."

Mildred is disappointed that none of the young Indian women of the tribe are interested enough or have the time to learn the traditional methods of making pottery. Recently she taught one young Pamunkey woman how to make handbuilt coil pots in the traditional method. Unfortunately, that woman moved off the reservation and no longer makes pottery. Now Mildred and Joyce "Pale Moon" Krigsvold are the only two Indian women still making hand built pottery on the

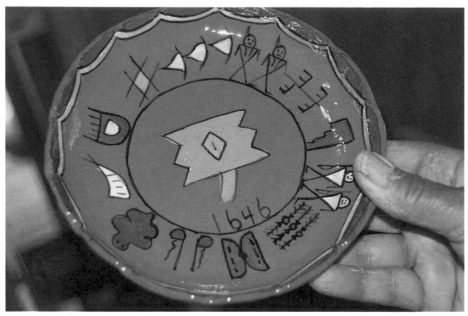

Mildred holds a plate she made decorated with pictographs that tell the story of the Treaty of 1646.

Pamunkey Reservation. Mildred signs her work with her Indian name, "Gentle Rain," and Joyce signs hers with her Indian name, "Pale Moon."

Because she is so interested in preserving the Pamunkey culture and learning cultural traditions from other tribes, she helped her daughter, Deborah "Little Wing" Moore, form the Intertribal Women's Circle. The group is comprised of women from many different tribes, and they share knowledge about art forms, as well as native traditions. The group also strives to encourage women to find ways to keep their heritage and traditions alive for future generations.

The coil method of making ceramics is the oldest pottery tradition among her people, and Mildred prefers making pots that way. She has been recognized as a Master Artist by the Virginia Folk Life Foundation and has given pottery making demonstrations for local, national, and international programs. The Valentine Richmond History Center, the Smithsonian National Museum of the American Indian in Washington, and universities and schools in England are some of the locations where she has shown people how she makes a coil pot.

Although the pottery made using the method taught at the Pottery School is not a tradition that is indigenous to Virginia, after so many years it could be considered a tradition among the Pamunkey. It illustrates a combining of cultural ideas. The fact that the Pamunkey also make pottery as their ancestors did using the coil method of construction illustrates how Indian cultural traditions have also been retained.

Chapter 7

✳

Zelma "Deer In Water" Wynn
Chickahominy Potter

There's excitement in her voice as Eliouse "Little Heart" Jones gently wipes the ashes off a pot that is still warm from the pit where it was fired. She shows it to her sister, Zelma Wynn, and says, "Look, this one has a little burgundy right down here near the bottom." Eliouse picks up another pot, "And this one has a little sparkle to it like someone added glitter near the top."

Zelma explains, "That's what makes pit firing so exciting, you never know how the pottery pieces will come out until you uncover them and wipe all the ashes off."

Some of the pieces have what are called "clouds," dark areas that show up against the white clay. Some of the "clouds" are larger and darker than others.

Zelma says, "There are no guarantees with pit firing. You can't be sure that a pot won't explode or break during the process. When the fire is going, and you hear a little pop you hold your breath hoping it was the wood popping and not a pot."

Because it is such a delicate process, Zelma and Eliouse and other modern Indians, fire their pieces in an electric kiln for a short period to make them stronger before they pit fire them. After the first firing the pieces are called bisque ware.

The women do try to stick as closely to traditional methods as they can, but they use matches rather than a fire stick and board to start the fire. Because of fire regulations they always consult the fire marshal before they do an outdoor firing. They also sit by the pit with a bucket of water and a hose at the ready should the fire get out of control.

Eliouse adds, "We have done it the old way without using a kiln, but that takes so much longer. You have to start off by drying the ground. And you don't

Zelma uses a cord wrapped paddle to add texture to a coil pot.

Zelma smoothes a coil pot.

put the pots directly into the fire even after the ground is warm. You build the fire and put the pots around it. Then you move the pots closer. They stay that way for a while and heat up a little bit, and then you move them closer and closer until eventually you get them in the fire. It took about 48 hours to do it that way, and we don't really have 48 hours to move the pots and watch the pit. Using the kiln first makes it so much faster, as well as safer, as far as breakage goes."

Before the clay pieces are fired, they dry until they get to what is called the leather hard stage. By that time they're firm enough to put designs on by scratching them into the clay. At that stage you can also take a deer antler and burnish, or rub, the pot until it takes on a slightly different color. After it is fired it will be a little shiny.

Eliouse uses a cord wrapped paddle to add texture to a pot.

"Now in the old days they might decorate the pieces by patting them with a cord-wrapped paddle to add texture to an area." Zelma explains, "To make a cord wrapped paddle you cut off a branch that is about the thickness of your thumb, or a little bigger, and peel the bark back. Then you take the part that you've peeled back and use a piece of shell or sharp deer antler to scrape the inside of it, and then twist it in your hands. That's how they made cordage, or rope. Then you take the cordage and wrap it around a flat piece of wood."

Zelma places a pot in the pit for firing or burning.

In building the fire they put pine tags, small branches and small pieces of wood and bark in the bottom of the pit so they'll have a base to put the clay objects on. After they put the clay pieces in the pit, they add wood and bark to cover the pots, masks, and small animals that they are firing.

Zelma places a mask in the pit for firing.

Zelma and her sister Eliouse place sticks on top of the pots for burning.

Zelma lights the fire to begin pit firing the clay pieces.

Eliouse covers the fire with a piece of metal so that the smoke will be contained around the pots.

Traditionally, Indians used clay that they got from a nearby river bank. But Zelma and Eliouse have not found a suitable source for clay so they use commercial clay, which is why it is white after the first firing. Zelma says, "The process for using native clay is quite involved, and if you haven't used clay from that area before, it might not be good for making pottery. There are several steps to go through before you find out if you can use it or not. We've tried digging clay from different places along the banks of the Chickahominy River, and we've checked the banks of the James River at Berkeley Plantation. We just haven't found a suitable source. A lady also gave me clay to try from another spot on the James River. After a hurricane part of the bank washed away. Her daughter lives in one of the houses there so she gave me clay to try to see if that would work, but it didn't. We've found that we can fuse part of that clay into commercial clay, but can't use it just by itself."

In talking about how they learned to make pottery, Zelma and Eliouse admit that most tribes in Virginia lost their pottery-making traditions because of the restrictions placed on Indians during Colonial times and in later years. To remedy this, about 30 or 50 years ago there was a program through the federal government that provided pottery classes to most of the tribes. Zelma says, "We had someone come to each site twice a week, and we heard from an archaeologist how pottery was made before the settlers came. That's how we reinvented doing pottery like our ancestors did. We learned exactly how our ancestors made their ceramic pieces because the archaeologists had analyzed the pieces of pottery they had found at different sites. Some of the pots had crushed shells mixed with the clay, and some pots had a certain amount of sand added to the clay. Different tribes in different areas used different combinations. Many of the pottery shards that the archaeologists found had a cord-wrapped paddle design on it. They also showed us a style of pot that is more oblong than round. The archaeologists called that style of pot Marcy Creek and said that was the earliest shape used in Virginia."

Eliouse adds, "When we make pottery the way our ancestors did, we don't use anything we haven't made ourselves."

To make a regular pot they start with a little round piece of clay. Zelma says, "You stick your fingers in the middle of the clay and make a little pinch pot. Then you add coils around and around the top of it until you get it to the height you want. I don't care how tall you want to make the pot; it all starts with a little pinch pot. It takes a good while to make a tall pot because you can only do so much, and then you have to stop and let it firm up. Then you can come back and add more to it. You keep it moist when not

Zelma carefully places a pot on a piece of cement to cool.

working on it by covering it with a wet cloth. Then when you start to work on it again, you do what is called scoring on the top of the pot. You take a sharp piece of bone or shell and mark all around the top. Then take slip, which is a mixture of clay and water, and add that on the top edge, where it acts as glue for the next coil. You don't have to use slip each time you add a coil, only when you've left it for a while, because the clay is usually moist enough for the coils to stick together once you start working. You keep on with the coils until it gets to the point

L to R. Zelma uses a shovel to remove the hot pieces from the fire pit while Eliouse steadies them with a rake.

Close-up of a pot being removed from the ashes after the pots have been burned.

After burning in the pit a pot has several dark areas or "clouds."

where it's not going to hold its shape, and then you have to stop for a while. As you add the coils, you smooth them out on the inside and outside so you don't see the shape of the coil. A lot of people use a shell, or piece of wood, or you can just use your hands to smooth it out."

Even when they make animals they start with a pinch pot. "For an animal you put two pinch pots together and take a coil and smooth it around both edges to make a hollow ball of clay. Then you make it into an animal or a bird. You can even put a small square hole in the bottom, or the end of the animal, and put another hole in it, and you can blow it like a whistle," says Zelma.

Their ancestors also made masks with clay. As Zelma explains it, "You take a flat piece of clay, sit in a chair, hold your head back, and put the clay over your face. The first thing you do is make a place for your mouth so you can breathe. Then you take your fingers and go over your eyebrows, your eyes, your cheekbones and your nose to define them in the clay. The mask is not supposed to look like the person who does it; instead, it represents your inner being. When you put the clay on your face, it feels nice and cool. I guess it's like a mud pack. Today women go to spas for facials, so it's not too different from that. You just leave the clay on long enough to get the features, and then you take it off. You hold it in your hand and sit something under it to cushion or support it until it gets almost hard. Most people put two holes in the top so the mask can be hung up. Some people decorate them with feathers after they have been fired, but they usually don't add any color."

During Pocahontas's time pottery making was one of the women's tasks, and the ceramic pieces were used for cooking or storage. When the Chickahominy reinvented doing pottery the traditional way, there were two older men who learned pottery making, too, but they have since passed away. Now it is mostly women making pottery again. Zelma and Eliouse have given classes to other members of the tribe, including a few men, who have wanted to learn the pottery making tradition.

A few years ago the tribe also got a grant to hold classes on Saturdays at the tribal center for children. The children leared the traditional crafts of pottery-making, beadwork, and leather work. Zelma says her first love is pottery, but because she was one of the few people who knew how to work with leather, she taught the children leather working.

Now she and Eliouse make regalia for other Indians out of buckskin. They have made regalia for the chief of their tribe, and chiefs of two other Virginia tribes. They are currently working on the regalia for the chief of the Eastern Chickahominy tribe.

When the young people talk about Indian School, they are talking about those classes that were held at the Tribal Center. When Zelma talks about Indian School she is talking about the school that she attended, Samaria Indian School. That school was an elementary school for Indian children which only went through the seventh grade.

A row of pots cool after being removed from the ashes of the hot fire.

Zelma's older siblings were not allowed to attend the white high school and were not particularly welcome at the black high school. There was no high school for Indians in the state. To attend high school they had to go to Bacone in Oklahoma. As Zelma remembers it, "The state gave each family $200 for a child to go to Bacone. That had to cover transportation out there, books and lodging while you were there, and everything."

Zelma attended high school in Virginia, but when she and her future husband decided they wanted to get married, they had to go to Washington, D.C., because the Racial Integrity Act was still in effect in Virginia, and to have "Indian" recorded as their race on their marriage certificate, they had to go out of state. The chief of the Chickahominy Tribe at that time was Oliver Adkins, and he went with them to Washington to make sure the paper work was correct. As with many descendants of the Powhatan tribes, they were proud of their heritage and would prefer to go to the trouble of going out of state to be married so they could retain their identity.

With the repeal of the Racial Integrity Act in 1968 things slowly changed for the better. In 1985 the tribe gained state recognition, but several years before that the sisters' success at making pottery the way their ancestors did had been recognized. Zelma and Eliouse gave demonstrations in many locations such as the Showplace in Richmond and at the Smithsonian Institution in Washington, D.C. Today they still help others make pieces out of clay and pass on their skills to members of the tribe when time allows.

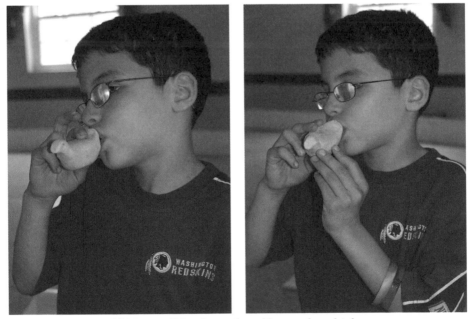

Dillon "Winter Hawk" Narron, Zelma's grandson, blows a clay whistle.

Chapter 8

Kelly "Autumn Dove" Adkins
Eastern Cherokee Bead Worker and Young Mother

Some of the children looked like they were flying. Whirling and jumping through the air with their fringes swinging gracefully, the children who were fancy dancers were agile and energetic. Also dancing to the same drum group were traditional dancers whose steps were more measured and very graceful. These children were in a group that presented Native American dances at the Governor's Conference on Indian Affairs in March of 1997. Some of the dances had been passed down from generation to generation, and the audience was delighted by the children's participation in that event.

Kelly Adkins holds one of the beaded pendants she has made.

But it was someone else who caught Kelly Adkins' eye when she attended that conference. She watched as Chickahominy Indian Troy Adkins received an award, and her girlfriend leaned over and said, "Now that's the kind of guy you ought to marry."

Kelly says, "I thought he was probably already married, but on the last night of the conference he asked me out. We went to Nacho Mamas, and then saw each other off and on for five months. I kept saying, 'Oh, we're just friends.' But we were married in December of 1998."

 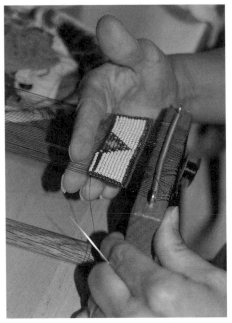

Kelly threading some beads on her needle.   *Close up of Kelly pushing a row of beads up to the rest of the project on the beading loom.*

She adds, "I had been on 'a searching' about my family, and about our heritage, and thought I might learn something at the conference. I am Eastern Cherokee from North Carolina on my mother's side. At that time I was dating someone in a drum group, and one of the members told me about the conference and sent me the registration form. I went with a girlfriend, but she had to leave that night, so I stayed Saturday by myself. It was a big step for me to go to something like that, and I found it really amazing. I had never seen anything like it."

Kelly is one of a number of Indian women who live in Virginia but are not from one of the eight state-recognized tribes. They are in Virginia for a variety of reasons. Sometimes they were born here; sometimes they have come to Virginia because of their jobs, other times they are in the military and stationed at Fort Lee, Fort A.P. Hill, or another Virginia base.

Some, like Kelly, marry an Indian who is from one of the state-recognized tribes. But there are also Indian women who marry someone who is non-Indian, or from another non state recognized tribe. These women are not descendants of Pocahontas's people, or the Powhatan tribes, but most still carry on Indian traditions, sometimes blending their own with the ones of the Powhatan descendants.

Kelly's tribe had seven clans. She says, "In our tribes the women were held in very high regard. The women were consulted before a war took place or before peace was declared. The tribes had a war chief and a peace chief, but they couldn't do anything until they consulted the women's council."

Her husband, Troy, grew up learning Chickahominy traditions. Kelly says, "Historically women were held in high regard in the Chickahominy tribe, too, but Troy is not sure if they really had a women's council or not."

Some of the information about the old ways was lost for various reasons by the Chickahominy. But a few of the traditions of both tribes are similar. Kelly says, "In some instances some of the ways the pottery was made are the same. In addition, the food eaten by the East Coast tribes was basically the same."

She goes on to say, "One thing Troy is very, very proud of is the fact that the Chickahominy were a warrior tribe, and they were one tribe that Powhatan could never get completely under his rule. But he always allied with them, so even though they weren't part of his confederacy, they were still friends. If Powhatan ever went to war, he always knew he wanted the Chickahominy to go forward with him. We always joke about the fact that his tribe was sort of feared. Troy says, 'The Cherokee never came over here; they knew better.' But I tell him, 'Yes they did.' I proved that to him after we got married and went to Peaks of Otter in Bedford County. We went walking and came upon this water hole that I had found, and there's a sign right there by the water hole that says, 'Cherokee and Siouan Waterhole. This is where the Cherokee and Sioux Indians would meet when they were coming back from hunting or a battle. They would meet here and stop to water their horses.' I thought that was absolutely amazing because I did not know the Sioux came this far East. But the Monacans, a Virginia tribe, are the only state recognized tribe that was not an Algonquian-speaking tribe, or under Powhatan. They were of Siouan descent, and in some ways I think the Cherokee could have become intermixed with the Monacan and Sioux because

Two beaded belts Kelly made. The one at the top is for her daughter Makayla's regalia; the other one is one she wore when she wore a Tear Dress.

One of Kelly's beaded pendants.

this was their hunting ground area."

Troy learned some of the traditional Chickahominy crafts and tried them himself. When he started dancing, he did some beading on his regalia. His wife says, "I asked him about the different stitches, and he said, 'Let me show you how this stitch is done.' So when we were making plans for our wedding, I wanted it traditional, but a Native wedding too, and said, 'I want beadwork in it.' Our bridesmaids all had something that had beadwork on it. I made the beadwork for the candles that they carried down the aisle. Troy did the beadwork on our candles – our unity candle, and also the candles on either side that we used to light the unity candle. Troy's sister-in-law beaded the pillow the ring bearer carried. She did a design on the pillow that was appliqué, a type of beadwork which is not done on a loom and is more free and curvy. It's a lot of what you would see in Ojibwa designs with flowers and things like that. I had been learning beadwork, but doing most of the work on a loom. An Ojibwa friend of mine showed me a little about appliqué beading, and he said that it wasn't really that hard but that it was a little more tedious."

Beadwork is an art form that is traditional with many tribes. Several people have taught her different aspects of beading. When she was working at NASA Langley Research Center in Hampton, Virginia, a friend of hers said he would teach her how to do beadwork on the loom. He took her to Home Depot and

One of Kelly's beaded pendants that is not finished and still on the beading loom.

Kelly working on the beading loom.

they bought the wood to make a loom. Kelly remembers, "We bought oak because I told him I wanted the best kind of wood. He bought the pieces to make two looms because he wanted to make one for himself too. Then he drew up a diagram and he said 'Your dad's good at building stuff so take these pieces home and see if he can put it together for you.'" Her father made the loom, but her friend went back to Oklahoma before he had time to teach her how to use it.

Later she had a roommate who was Cherokee, and she told Kelly she could show her how to do beading on the loom. Kelly says, "She showed me how to string up the loom and showed me the basic things to do with the beads. I sat down and started working and loved it. I was in that apartment

Both children dressed in their regalia with Kelly.

for two more weeks, and from the time that she showed me until I left, every night I was in my room doing beadwork.

Mikayla Adkins does a few dance steps in her regalia. She wears a Tear Dress.

Jordan Adkins in his Traditional Men's regalia.

Troy, Kelly and Mikayla in a Circle Dance at the VITAL powwow held at the Chickahominy Tribal Grounds.

To do the loomwork, the number of beads needed for the row are picked up on the needle and then pushed onto the thread. Then the threaded beads are brought up under the threads on the loom. The beads are then pushed up through those threads. Next the needle is run through the beads on top of the threads on the loom. When the thread is pulled through the beads they are attached to the work on the loom. Then that row of beads is pushed up against the rest of the piece. Kelly says, "The hardest part is when you start because you have to make sure each bead is pushed up. If all the beads are not pushed up when you run the needle through, a bead will sink down, and there will be a dip in your work. Once you've done it for a while, it's really very simple. It's one of the most relaxing things for me to do."

Now that Kelly and Troy have two children it's a little harder for her to find time to devote to beadwork, especially since she is home-schooling five-year-old Jordan and four-year-old Mikayla. But when they are taking a nap or in bed for the night, she sits down at the loom and works.

She often makes pendants that she designed herself before she got married. As she says, "I saw a design I liked and thought I could add to it. I started playing around with it and drew it up. It was horizontal. I thought, 'What if I made it vertical and long enough to be a pendant that can hang down with fringe on the bottom? When I first started out I had to draw out each design on bead paper, and color each space where a bead would be. Now I have it in my head, but if I get stuck and am not sure how many beads go in the next row, I look at a finished pendant or design on bead paper and count the beads in that row and then go back and do it on the loom."

Troy, Kelly and Mikayla in a Circle Dance.

"The first pendant I made was for my mom. I came up with the design, and then came up with a way to do the fringe. Usually you run the thread through the beads and then around the last bead and back up through the beads for the fringe, but that makes it kind of stiff, so I came up with the idea of using glue. I put a drop on the end and then hold the thread up so it runs back through the beads. When it's dry I can move it around and loosen the glue. Then I snip off the tips of the thread that hangs off the very end so it's flush with the beads. Then it is flexible enough that it sways when the person moves. I've always wanted the fringe to sway the way grass or shawl fringe sways in the wind."

Kelly has done a lot of other beaded things too. She made the side panels for her son Jordan's regalia and his cuffs. She also made side panels and cuffs for Troy's regalia and belts for Mikayla and herself. She has also beaded moccasins and is in the process of making hair ties and learning how to make earrings.

There are many different kinds of beads. She says, "I've just learned about cut beads. I used them on my son's side panels and cuffs. There are three cuts on the bead so they reflect the light. When you're dancing it's really awesome to see them sparkle. The one thing I don't like to use is plastic beads. For the neckpieces of the pendants, I use bone or buffalo horn and glass crow beads. I always try to use something natural."

People have bought some of Kelly's pendants at Fort Cherokee outside Williamsburg, Virginia, and she has given several away as gifts. She made one for the chief of the Nansemond tribe, Chief Bass, and one for another member of that tribe, Nita Smith.

Each pendant has at least five colors, and if someone asks her to do a pendant, she asks them to tell her five colors they like. With those colors she'll sit down and look at a pendant she's already done and say "I'm going to put this color here and this color here. I love to see the design come out, but sometimes when I get the first couple of lines on there I think, 'I don't know if I like this.' And then I'll ask Troy who will say, 'Well, do a couple more lines.' And when I do a few more lines I find that I like it. And when it comes out, it's even more beautiful than I first thought it would be."

Beautiful as it is, her beadwork is more than just decorative and pretty to wear. Kelly says, "I've made pendants for several people and each one is different, so every time the person looks at it and wears it they know that I'm praying for them. I want them to know that my hands were used as an instrument of the Holy Spirit to make the pendant just for them. I can remember the design I made for them and I can sit there and pray, 'Lord, I remember who this person is and I pray that you would continue to be with them, wherever they are, whatever they do, whatever they say that it would be for your Glory and that you would be able to move in them.' I pray over every bead that goes on the loom. And I pray over the wearer of the pendant. I pray that they would have eyes to see and ears to hear the voice of the Lord speaking to them. That's my mission field in a way. I can touch people through my beadwork from my home in a way that I can't by going out to them."

Kelly adds, "And if the person is a dancer I pray that the Lord would be with them as they dance and that the dancing would be able to minister to people. Dancing is not just about being out there to show off, it's a message, and the dancer's focus should be vertical towards the heavens not horizontal with what's going on around. The circle is our church, and we dance to glorify the Creator—

Kelly in her Fancy Dancer's regalia.

not to entertain."

If Kelly is not interrupted, she can do half of a pendant on the loom in one day. Usually if the children are outside playing, she might work on the loom and get to do five or six lines. She has to work her beadwork around household chores and the children's schedule which includes home schooling.

"I've been working with them since they were two or three, and they are ahead of where they would be if they were in public schools. I enjoy taking them to places and teaching them about things they are curious about. There's a lot of controversy about the public schools today, and I like to be able to have more control over what my children learn. When the door closes on the public school sometimes you don't know what's going on. Here I have the ability to control that.

My children have about 45 minutes each morning for Bible study. They can learn stories from the Bible and their Bible verses. We do the pledge of Allegiance to the American flag and the Christian flag, and I can control that. In public school they would not have the ability to learn about the Bible. I also believe in my heart, based upon my faith, it is of the Lord for me to be able to teach them the standards and the morals that they need. I want to be the one to teach them about human sexuality. I believe it should be, 'These are the standards, and you don't do this until you have this ring and this paper.'"

Also with home schooling it gives them more free time, and more time with me. It would break my heart to send them off on a bus and watch them drive

Kelly in her Fancy Dancer's regalia does a Fancy Dancer's Shawl Dance.

Copywrite Teresa Koren,
The Valentine Richmond's History Center

The Troy Adkins family at a presentation at the Valentine Richmond History Center. Back: Kelly and Troy, front: Mikayla and Jordan.

away, or walk into a school building behind closed doors where I don't know what's going on. They are such a part of my life. I tell them every day they are the sunshine in my day."

The children are full of questions. Kelly says, "We went to Jamestown recently and Werowocomoco last year. I was telling them about Powhatan and the Powhatan Confederacy. They saw a fire pit where they would cook and also pieces of pottery, so they are already learning about their heritage even at this young age. They also ask questions about the Indian things we have here. I have literature that I show them, and they learn from that. Some of the traditions of Troy's tribe are a little different from my tribe, so I'm trying to teach them about both."

Mikayla and Jordan have been going to powwows and seeing traditional Indian dancing since they were very young. Each member of the family wears a different type of regalia. Troy wears the men's traditional made of buckskin with a feather bustle. Kelly used to wear traditional regalia made from cotton. A Cherokee woman made her first regalia for her, and it was called a Cherokee Tear Dress. The name comes from the fact that on the Trail of Tears women would make clothing and blankets from fragments of cloth that they tore. Since they were made out of torn cloth they were called tear dresses. Over the years they started to call it the Tear Dress in remembrance of the Trail of Tears. After she had her children, Kelly decided to do fancy shawl dancing, so now her regalia is made of bright fabrics with appliquéd designs, and she dances with a shawl with long fringe. Troy made Jordan buckskin pants that he wears with a ribbon shirt, and Mikayla wears a tear dress just like her mother's first regalia.

Although she has two pendants started on the beading loom, Kelly is already looking forward to her next projects. She plans to make beaded cuffs to add to her daughter's regalia.

Chapter 9

✳

Melanie Wright
Creek Indian and Historic Interpreter

Melanie Wright reached into her basket of garden tools and gave Amy Little a piece of tree branch that was shaped like a hoe. She showed her how Powhatan Indians would have cultivated their garden in the 17th Century. It was not too long before Amy was ready to stop because it was hard work turning the soil on a hot, humid summer day. It made Amy and others watching realize how hard early Virginia Indian women had to work.

Tia Lee felt the same way when she tried her hand at scraping the fur off a deer skin that was stretched on a frame in front of the recreated yehawken in the Arrohatoc Village, the recreated Indian area of Henricus Historical Park in Chesterfield County, Virginia. After scraping a small area with a shell, she had removed some fur, but could not imagine how hard it would be to clean the whole hide.

These are some of the hands-on activities that Melanie Wright encourages visitors to Henricus to try. This allows them to get a feel for the daily tasks that Indian women who lived during the time of Chief Powhatan and his daughter, Pocahontas, had to perform at different times during the year.

Melanie is a Creek Indian, and her ancestors spoke the Muskogean language rather than the Algonquian language that the Powhatan Indians spoke. But the Creeks were Eastern Woodland Indians, just as the Powhatan Indians were, so there are some similarities between the tribes. Melanie says, "You have Oklahoma Creeks who were removed from the East Coast during the Trail of Tears, and then you have Georgia and Alabama Creeks, who escaped the Trail of Tears.

In period dress, or traditional Indian clothing, Melanie interprets the 17th Century way of life of the Indian tribes that lived near Henricus, the second English settlement in the New World and where Pocahontas was held captive for a period of time. There is some discussion about whether Pocahontas actually lived at Henricus or whether she lived across the river with Reverend Whitaker and his family. But there is no question about the fact that she learned English ways and was converted to Christianity by Reverend Whitaker. She probably met John Rolfe in the area, too. After their marriage, which took place at Jamestown, Pocahontas was called Lady Rebecca, and she and her husband lived at Varina which is not far from Henricus. Melanie thinks it is safe to say that at one time or another Pocahontas walked the grounds where the reconstructed Henricus now stands.

It is difficult to dispel misconceptions about the early Powhatan tribes, and sometimes Melanie finds it discouraging to find instructional material stating that all early Virginia Indians lived in longhouses. While some say that was the English name for the Indian dwellings, others contend that the longhouse was a dwelling for more than one family and is more of a Northern Iroquois or Northern Algonquian type of structure. In *First People: The Early Indians of Virginia* by Keith Egloff and Deborah Woodward, an illustration shows two styles of Late Woodland homes. It states that Longhouses were shared by up to 20 family members, while smaller domed houses were occupied by smaller family groups. The smaller domed houses covered with sewn mats were called yehawkens by the Powhatans, and that is the type of house that Melanie interprets at Henricus. She also finds it ironic that the Powhatan Indians were said to use birch bark canoes. As she says, "How could they have birch bark canoes? It's

very rare that you see the type of birch tree that was used to make canoes down here. They probably would have liked to have birch bark canoes because they are lighter than the dugout canoes they made, but I don't think they had any."

Melanie beginning a basket that she will twine.

Close-up of left.

And as to the use of the term "how" as a greeting she says, "That was not used around here. It's a Siouan greeting and it's more of a passive saying like "hey." "Wingapo" is the accepted Powhatan form of greeting." Melanie likes to teach school children who visit the site that word. She also teaches them "kenah" which means thank you and

Melanie with the end of a weaver on her bone needle.

"anah" which means goodbye. Most of the Algonquian language has been forgotten because it was not written down, and during Colonial times, Indians were forbidden to use their language, although a few words have survived.

She says that young people have made some progress in eliminating some of the stereotypes. "They've gotten to know that we didn't have horses, but then you have to convince them that there weren't any farm animals. There were no chickens, cows, goats, or sheep. I think it's difficult to teach children what was available for the early Indians to use. It's hard for them to understand that only some plants and animals that we know today were indigenous to this land before Europeans started visiting our shores."

The most frequently asked question is, "Is it real?" Melanie says, "They see the deer skin, the bones, and they want to know if they're real. We live in such a 'Disneyfied' society that unfortunately when they come out here they think

Melanie works the ends of the weavers into the basket using a bone needle to finish the basket.

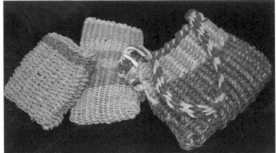

Three flat baskets made by Melanie.

Two baskets made by Melanie.

everything is fake, too, just like it is at *Disney*. And that's very, very sad. I also think it's incredibly upsetting that when we have school children see the chickens from the English settlement, they don't think they're real. They say, 'That's not chicken.' When you ask them why they say, 'Cause chicken is in a package from the grocery store.'"

When they learn that she is a real Indian, some ask her if she's an Indian princess. For some reason they think all Indian girls were princesses. Because they expect her to look like the stereotype of an Indian, they even question her curly hair.

Melanie says, "I was born and raised in Virginia. I attended Virginia

Commonwealth University and got a degree in Museum Studies. I knew I wanted to focus on Eastern Woodland Indians because of my ties to them. I began working at the Jamestown Settlement, and worked there for three years.

Unfortunately I was not raised in an Indian environment at all. My grandmother was raised in Georgia in a time when you were better off being anything but Indian. She would lie and tell people we were something else. When she moved to Key West Florida, she tried telling everybody the family was Cuban even though she didn't speak Spanish."

She goes on to say, "My father remembers when she was walking him to a rest room in Key West and someone walked up and jumped in front of her and told her she

Melanie with the basket she made using natural dyes and fibers to hold her fire making tools.

wasn't allowed to use that bathroom. She didn't understand, and they said, 'That's for whites only.' So it was a difficult time. Then the black community was saying 'Well, they're not black either.' It was like a double-edged sword. You're not this, but you're not that either. And Georgia was very harsh on the Indian community, especially during Andrew Jackson's time and the Trail of Tears. In Georgia they only accepted two races – white or "colored" just like the state of Virginia did for a while, but those in Georgia who were not white had to deal with that for a lot longer. So it's very hard to prove your heritage through documentation. If you were an Indian you were listed as colored. They were pretty cruel to Indians."

Melanie learned several Indian crafts at Jamestown. She says, "They put you with someone who taught you different skills, and I was very fortunate that the people they put me with in each one of the trades were the best ones they could have. One was a Chippewa woman, and she taught me how to do most of the weaving that I learned."

Weaving is done with cordage. What we would call rope, or string, today was called cordage by the English in the 17th Century. Melanie says, "Cordage could be made out of any kind of plant fiber that was long and stringy enough to twist into rope. I have yucca rope, bark rope, sea grass rope. It just depended on where the people were and what resources nature provided them with."

The pointed type of basket that Powhatan Indians made showing the bottom pushed up so that it can sit on a flat surface.

One of the types of weaving that Melanie learned and demonstrates at Henricus is finger weaving or Indian braiding. Long pieces are woven and used as belts and basket handles as well as tump lines. Tump lines are what Northern and Eastern Woodland and Algonquian Indians used to put across their foreheads, and tie in the back so they could carry something on their backs. Melanie comments, "Anything that had to be long was probably finger woven."

She uses several types of cordage and makes most of her own. She colors it using natural dyes like pokeberries, which come from what most people consider a weed. Pokeberries give the cordage a nice rose color, but it does fade after time. To begin finger weaving she chooses several pieces of long cordage and ties them into a knot. So that the pattern shows better she uses two different colors. One piece serves as the anchor piece and she goes over and back and through the center and then switches. Melanie says, "There are ways of mixing the strands up to come out with a different pattern. You can do a chevron design or blocks of color."

According to Melanie, Powhatan Indians sometimes wove a basket with a pointed bottom. They made pots for cooking with pointed bottoms, so that would be the same style, just a different material. She says, "I have manipulated the ones with pointed bottoms so that they sit flat by pushing the inner part in. The early Indians made baskets like that and put corn kernels in them to trade corn with the English. But when they traded corn in that type of basket and it was sitting on a flat surface, the Englishmen didn't realize that the center part was pushed inward. They thought the bottom was flat and that whole basket was filled with corn. As they emptied the corn out, they found that part of the basket had been pushed in and took up space, and the corn was more or less just around the edges and across the top. It's easy to imagine that the English got upset because they felt as if they had been cheated."

The type of basket that Melanie is currently working on will have a flat bottom and the process she is using is called twining. She says, "Basically you start at the bottom and work your way up and around. The centerpieces are called the spokes and you start with two sets. One set goes one way and one set comes across the other way. In twining the long pieces are called the weavers, and you twine your weaver around your spokes so you separate them."

As she talks, she twines weavers around the spokes on a 12-spoke basket. She says, "I've got them separated into six and six spokes, so I go around the six for a while, and then separate them out into fours, and then I'll separate them out into twos. Once you get to working with one at a time the basket will flip up all by itself, and that will be the sides of the basket. In this one I'm using two different fibers. One is hemp and one is jute. Hemp is stiffer, and jute is more pliable, so I'm using that as my weaver because I can manipulate that more easily and you have to twist, then pull the weavers through. You can also make a flat basket almost the same way. Instead of it being round you just fold it in half, but you still do the weaving in the same way – you're still twisting and pulling through, but you don't start with groups of spokes, you just work with single spokes. To finish it I have to use a flat bone needle to poke the ends of the spokes back down through the sides."

Melaine next describes the process used to produce roofs for early houses. The mats used for this may appear to be woven but are not. Melanie says, "Mats were actually sewn together out of cattails. Because cattails are spongy, when they get wet they swell, so if you've got a lot of cattails lined up in a row and you weave around them or twine around them it creates a small hole the size of the thickness of the cordage between them. So that hole, even though

Melanie outside the yehawken at Henricus.

Melanie holds a sharpened shell to scrape the fur off the deer skin.

L to R. Tia Lee and Tim Pleasants listen to Melanie explain how Powhatan women prepared a deer hide.

With a yehawken in the background Melanie explains to Tia Lee how the Powhatan Indians used the tendon from the leg of a deer to make sinew and the bones to make tools.

it's small is going to create a leak, but if you sew through the cattail into its next partner, there are no holes because there's no cordage around it. When it gets wet the cattails push up against each other, and it's water tight. We found this out by doing it at Jamestown when I worked there. We made cattail mats and when we got them wet we could see them swell. Then in the 17th Century when there would be a fire constantly burning in the yehawken, that would cause them to dry out once it stopped raining. The cattails would shrink back down causing the house to be able to breathe again and letting a lot of the smoke out of the house."

The early Powhatan Indians used bone needles to sew the cattails together, and Melanie has made several types of bone tools and needles. Just as today, there are different needles for different tasks. She says, "Archaeologists have actually found bone needles at different sites. But that's very unusual because bone tools are all biodegradable and usually disintegrate over the years. What archaeologists have found is that a deer's rib bones were split to make special bone needles for sewing the mats on the yehawken. The whole rib bone can be separated into two pieces. One part is not pliable, but the other part will bend. After digging the marrow out of the bone and drilling a hole in one end with a sharp flake of stone, they had something like our curved upholsterer's needles. If they were sewing a mat onto the yehawken, they could stick the needle in and it curved and came back out. Therefore you did not have to stand on the inside and have someone else on the other side poking the needle back to you. A woman

Melanie shows Amy Little how to use a hoe in the Indian garden at Henricus.

Melanie shows Amy Little some of the tools in her garden basket. Amy is holding a planting stick.

could do light repair work by herself on the mats if her husband was away."

One thing Melanie learned at Henricus is that making bone tools is easier if the bones are fresh. She says, "We cooked a bunch of deer ribs, and as soon as the meat was done and taken off the bones, we started in on the bone tools."

The bone needles go through cattails, but not through leather. Melanie explains, "That's why you have an awl to poke the holes in the leather. The sewing thread was sinew. That's a tendon, usually a deer leg tendon, and when it is pounded with a smooth stone, it separates into many fibers which you can either twist up into rope or use one fiber to sew with. It's very strong and will last a long time. Needles were probably not used for sewing leather pieces together. Because it is so stiff, you can push it through the holes made with the awl. Sinew was also used for bow strings. The back strap tendon, the one that runs from the neck to the tail in the deer, or any animal, is the best one to use because it is the longest one. That one works very well for bow strings."

As for Melanie's own family heritage – she is still searching. She remembers her great grandfather, who was full-blooded Creek, as looking like what most people think Indians look like. He was very dark in color and had higher cheekbones and what she calls "squinty eyes." She says, "He never talked about who he was or what he did, so unfortunately he took that to the grave with him. My grandmother still won't talk about being Indian. I'm the only one she will discuss any of this with because of what I do for a living. I'm also the only one in the family who has actually shown a major interest in our heritage. Only recently has she started to give me information so that I can start looking back a lot more genealogically. I've wanted to find out what particular tribe we belonged to in Georgia. The Oklahoma Creeks took so much of their culture with them. That was all they had to take with them, and they still can tell what tribe they were from. All I know is that we were part of the Lower Creeks. The Lower Creeks were in lower Georgia, and the Upper Creeks were in northern Alabama. And we know that there were about 14 different tribes in our group. It was very similar to the 32 tribes considered part of Powhatan's chiefdom. I wanted to find out which tribe we belonged to, and my grandmother said she had no idea which one it was. So I'm trying to look back in my great grandfather's records and find documentation. I had no idea what I was getting into. It takes a lot of work."

Although she doesn't know a lot about her own tribe, she does know a lot about Powhatan history, and Melanie says, "I like doing what the women did – cordage-making, basket-making, mat-making, cooking, and fleshing and tanning the deer hides.

It seems the movie *The New World* has prompted a lot of interest in Virginia Indians and the way they lived. I was asked to be in that movie, but I knew that all they wanted to do was make a blockbuster movie, and that they were not all that interested in portraying the Powhatan culture accurately. So I said 'No' because my job is to interpret Powhatan life, and I can't turn around and disrespect that way of life by being in a movie that is not completely accurate."

Glossary

Algonquian – A family of languages spoken by North American Indian people including the Powhatan group. The particular language spoken by the Powhatans is extinct except for a few words.

Bisque – The first firing of clay objects or pottery - usually in a kiln. After this firing they may be glazed and fired again, or as Native Americans do with their traditional pottery, they may be fired in a pit, or burned.

Chief Emeritus – An honorary title for a former Indian chief.

Cordage – The 17th Century term for rope or string

Documentary genocide – The systematic attempt to destroy an ethnic group by creating false documents, or writing down false information for future generations.

Dugout canoe – Burning and then scraping the burnt material out of a log to create a canoe. The type of canoe typically created by the Powhatan Indians.

Federal Recognition – In regard to Indians it refers to the recognition by the government of the United States of a tribe, which confers upon that tribe certain sovereign rights. There are three ways for Indian tribes to attain Federal Recognition: through the Bureau of Indian Affairs, by an act of Congress, and legal actions through the court systems. Six of the state-recognized tribes in Virginia are currently seeking historical Federal Recognition through two separate acts now being considered by Congress.

Indigenous – Native to a country or region. People, plants or animals that were established in a particular area in prehistoric times.

Longhouse – The English term for an Eastern Woodlands Indian house. Currently historians distinguish between a longhouse, built to hold several families, and a yehawken built for only one family.

Matoaca – The Indian name of the daughter of Chief Powhatan, most commonly known as Pocahontas. Other spellings include: Mataoaka, Matoax, or Matowaka.

Matriarchal – A society in which family descent and inheritance are passed through the mother rather than the father.

Pictographs - Pictures or designs used by early Indians on walls, and later, used to decorate pottery. They often tell a story.

Powhatan – The term for the head chief, or ruler, of a number of Indian tribes in Central and Tidewater Virginia. The term is also used for the members of those tribes, as in The Powhatan People. It was also the Native American name for the river that is now called the James River, and it was the name of the tribe that was located on that river near what is now Richmond.

Powwow – A gathering of Indian people. Today it is an event which is usually highlighted by Native American, or Indian, drumming and dancing in a special dance circle.

Racial Integrity Law – A law passed by the Virginia General Assembly in 1924. Those who supported the law were racial purists, and recognized only two races: white and colored. As far as the law and its supporters were concerned there were no Indians in Virginia as they did not recognize "Indian" as a race. Many Indians were classified as "colored." It was struck down by the United States Supreme Court in 1968.

Regalia – Special clothing worn by Native Americans, or American Indians. It is considered a personal statement of who they are by many Indians. Traditional regalia is often made of buckskin, but there are many variations.

State Recognition – Indian tribes that meet certain criteria are given state recognition. Different states have different criteria, and a tribe can only be recognized in one state. In Virginia there are eight state recognized tribes whose members are descendants of tribes indigenous to Virginia that are currently located in approximately the same areas as they were at the time of the arrival of European settlers. John Smith's 1624 map is used to compare their early locations with their current ones.

Trail of Tears – A culturally devastating event for Southeastern Indians, primarily the Cherokees, Chickasaws, Choctaws, Creeks, and Seminoles, who were forcibly removed from their homes, and moved by land and water routes hundreds of miles to a new home in Oklahoma Indian Territory. Some say gold was found in Georgia, and that prompted the removal. It became national policy to move Indians west of the Mississippi River after the Louisiana Territory was purchased form the French in 1803. Some Creeks in Georgia and Alabama escaped, and still live there today, along with some of the Eastern Cherokees who lived in North Carolina. Indians living in Virginia, and parts of North Carolina and South Carolina were spared.

Twining – A method of weaving used by Virginia Indians.

Yehawken - A domed dwelling formed by bending saplings into an arch, then covered with sewn mats. Typically a single family house used by Eastern Woodlands Indians.

Resources

BOOKS –
First People: The Early Indians of Virginia
By Keith Eglofff and Deborah Woodward
University Press of Virginia
Charlottesville, Virginia (1992)

Pocahontas's People: The Powhatan Indians of Virginia Through Four Centuries
By Helen Rountree
University of Oklahoma Press, Norman Oklahoma (1989)

We're Still Here: Contemporary Virginia Indians Tell Their Stories
Sandra Waugaman and Danielle Moretti-Langholtz, Ph.D.
Palari Publishing
PO Box 9288
Richmond, Virginia 23227 (2000 – revised 2006)

MUSEUMS –
Henricus – The 1611 Citie of Henricus
Chesterfield County at Dutch Gap
(804) 705-1340

Historic Crab Orchard Museum and Pioneer Park
Rt. 1, P.O. Box 194
Tazewell, VA 24651
(540) 988-6755

Historic Jamestowne
Colonial Parkway
Williamsburg, VA
(757) 898-2410

Jamestown Settlement
PO Box 1607
Williamsburg, VA 23187
(757) 229-1607

Monacan Indian Village at Natural Bridge
Exits 175 & 180 off I-81
(804) 533-1410 or (540) 291-1038

Pamunkey Indian Museum
175 Lay Landing Rd.
King William, VA 23086
(804) 843-4792

Smithsonian National Museum of the American Indian
Fourth St. and Independence Ave. S.W.
Washington, DC 20560
(202) 633-1000

Virginia Historical Society
428 N Boulevard
Richmond, VA 23221
(804) 358-4901

Virginia Museum of Natural History
1001 Douglas Avenue
Martinsville, VA 24112
(540) 666-8600

Wolf Creek Indian Village and Museum
Rt.1, Box 1530
Bastian, VA 24314
(540) 688-3438

WEB SITES –
Virginia Council on Indians and links to the eight state recognized tribes
www.Indians.vipnet.org

The American Indian Resource Center at the College of William & Mary
www.wm.edu/airc

Jamestown Settlement – Jamestown-Yorktown Foundation
www.historyisfun.org

Historic Jamestown – The National Park Service and AVPA Preservation Virginia
www.Historic.Jamestown.org

Native Arts
www.nativearts.com

OTHERS
The Pepperbird Foundation –
PO Box 1071,
Williamsburg, VA 23187
(767)220-5761
Educational programs, and publishes Pepperbird Pathways: American Indian
Heritage, a list of Virginia powwows and resources. Distributed through the
Virginia Tourism Corp, and available at Virginia Tourism Welcome Centers.

Index